Employee Assistance Programs in South Africa

∞ ALL HAWORTH BOOKS & JOURNALS
ARE PRINTED ON CERTIFIED
ACID-FREE PAPER

Employee Assistance Programs in South Africa

R. Paul Maiden
Editor

The Haworth Press, Inc.
New York • London • Norwood (Australia)

Employee Assistance Programs in South Africa has also been published as *Employee Assistance Quarterly*, Volume 7, Number 3 1992.

The Haworth Press, Inc., 10 Alice Street, Binghamton, NY 13904-1580, USA

Library of Congress Cataloging-in-Publication Data

Employee assistance program in South Africa / R. Paul Maiden, editor.
p. cm.
Includes bibliographical references.
ISBN 1-56024-302-3 (alk. paper)
1. Employee assistance programs–South Africa. I. Maiden, R. Paul.
HF5549.5.EA42E49 1992
331.25–dc20 92–12236
CIP

Employee Assistance Programs in South Africa

Employee Assistance Programs in South Africa

CONTENTS

Employee Assistance Programs in South Africa

ABOUT THE EDITOR

R. Paul Maiden is Chair of the Occupational Social Work Program at the Jane Addams College of Social Work, The University of Illinois at Chicago. He also serves as Research Associate at the Jane Addams Center for Social Policy and Research and is Consulting Director for Managed Care Services for Perspectives, Ltd., a Chicago-based employee assistance and managed mental health care firm. Mr. Maiden has been in the EAP field for thirteen years and has published extensively in the areas of AIDS in the workplace, EAP evaluation, and ethics and EAPs. A licensed clinical social worker and certified employee assistance professional, he is currently completing a PhD at the University of Maryland. Mr. Maiden was born in Zimbabwe, Africa and is a naturalized U.S. citizen.

Foreword

At 7 a.m. on August 15, 1991, I arrived in Johannesburg to start a 15 day visit to The Republic of South Africa. Over the next two weeks I visited some 18 South African cities and towns and traveled more than 2,000 miles within the country.

South Africa is a surprisingly attractive place. It is a lovely country that is highly developed by world standards. It has many of the best characteristics of the United States (USA) forty or fifty years ago. It has unspoiled beaches and landscapes, a good infrastructure of highways, airlines and passenger trains. It is a relatively safe country, and its people are friendly toward North Americans. The cities of South Africa are as beautiful, well-developed and cultural as most cities of comparable size in the Northern Hemisphere. The sea shores around Cape Town and Durban are superior to those of California and Florida. The Drakensburg Mountains and the other mountain chains of South Africa are as breathtaking and awe-inspiring as the Rockies or Appalachian Mountains. The high veld around Johannesburg reminds one of Oklahoma, West Texas or even Kansas or Nebraska.

According to the 1991-92 South Africa Official Yearbook, South Africa has historically been viewed as a geographic designation rather than the reflection of a national reality. In fact, the country came into being not because of any natural affinity between its inhabitants but rather under the sextant and compass of British imperialism. Apart from the White community of both Dutch and British, lines were arbitrarily drawn that incorporated Black groups such as Xhosas, Zulus Swazi, Basuto and Tswana within their own clearly defined territories.

There is also a large racially-mixed community of "Coloureds," mostly the product of miscegenation between indigenous Khoikhoi, White settlers and Blacks. The four major ethnic divisions are the Nguni, Sotho, Shangaan-Tsonga and Venda. Together, the Nguni and Sotho account for the largest percentage of the Black population.

The Nguni language group comprises three sub-groups: Zulus with approximately 7.6 million people, Xhosas with approximately 3 million and a smaller group, the South Ndebele. The Sotho group of 7.6 million also comprises several sub-groups: North Sotho, South Sotho and Twansas.

The Tsonga, also known as the Shangaan-Tsonga account for another 1.5 million Black South Africans while the Venda is the smaller of the groups with 200,000. These groups make up tribes that are estimated to approach 1,000 in number. In June 1990, the number of Black people in South Africa totalled 21.6 million.

Of the 5 million Whites in South Africa, an estimated 56 percent are Afrikaans speaking. The Afrikaaner traces his origins to the Dutch East India Company settlement at the Cape in 1652. The ethnic composition of the Afrikaner is estimated to be 40 percent Dutch, 40 percent German, 7.5 percent French, 7.5 percent English and Scots and 5 percent other. Approximately 38 percent of the 5 million Whites are English speaking.

There are 3.2 million Coloureds with approximately 85 percent living in the Cape Province. They also include two subcultures—the Griquas and the Cape Malays. There are approximately 956,000 Asians. Of this group, 938,700 are estimated to be Indians, 12,600 Chinese, 500 Japanese and 4,200 other Asians.

English and Afrikaans are South Africa's two official languages. Afrikaans had its beginning in 1652 when the Dutch language was transplanted to the new colony at the southern tip of Africa where it became the official language. Within 150 years of the establishment of the Dutch settlement, the Dutch language was supplanted by Afrikaan, the only dramatic language to have originated outside Europe. Afrikaans was accepted as an official language by an Act of Parliament in 1925. South Africa is the only country in the world where Afrikaans is spoken.

Fanakalo is a pidgin language developed in the mines where the numerous different languages spoken by Black workers soon created a need for a common language that could easily be learned by everyone. Fanakalo is a conglomerate language of Zulu, English and Afrikaans. It serves the general purpose but is considered an inferior and undignified language by Black South Africans.

It becomes quickly evident that South Africa has one of the most complex and diversified population mixes in the world. This is underscored by the fact that none of South Africa's 11 major languages is spoken by a majority of all the people. These cultural, ethnic, tribal and language variations have set the scene for the current political landscape.

South Africa is a misunderstood nation. There has been racial segregation and racial strife just as there has been in the United States. However, petty apartheid-segregated facilities no longer exist and considerable progress has been made in ending job segregation and housing segregation. Even in Soweto, a black city with a population of metropolitan Cleveland, a close observer will find beautiful homes, creative talent at work, and burgeoning black capitalism. There are areas in need of improvement, such as squatter's camps, but nowhere are the problems in South Africa on a scale with those in Mexico or Latin America. If you have been afraid to travel to South Africa because of perceived racial unrest, be assured that it is safer to travel to South Africa than to Washington, D.C., Atlanta, GA, or New York City.

I was given an opportunity to spend three days looking closely at the Employee Assistance Program at the Electric Supply Commission of South Africa (ESKOM). This program is managed by Chris Van Der Heever, a member of the Employee Assistance Society of North America (EASNA). I found the ESKOM EAP to be a mature, well managed program. Their EAP team is currently engaged in a cost-benefit analysis study that the *EAQ* hopes to publish later this year.

On Saturday, August 16, 1991, Mr. Van Der Heever drove me to their Duvha power station, some 90 minutes east of Johannesburg. The Duvha power station is built next to a coal mine. It is an enormous power plant where more than thirteen hundred people work. It is fully computerized and a single cooling tower could hold the largest hotel in South Africa. The smokestack at the Duvha plant is the highest man made structure in the southern hemisphere.

ESKOM uses the cultural center adjacent to the power plant center to create better working relationships between the diverse cultural and ethnic groups within the company.

The cultural center is in a Kraal or round fenced area within which a clan has traditionally lived. The Duvha Kraal is unique in that it contains representative homes of a dozen different tribes. Each home contains the traditional cultural objects of that tribe—cooking utensils, articles of clothing, religious objects, and games. These homes are used to teach workers of all races and groups about the culture of others.

There is a common hall where work groups meet to eat and study. Meals are often used as learning opportunities. While employees are asked to eat in traditional African ways, African tribesmen from the homelands are invited to eat with formal dinner settings.

Functions such as this are seen as a part of the EAP's responsibility in ESKOM, as are such normal functions as helping to solve the personal problems of employees whose personal problems are having an adverse effect on attendance and productivity.

While we were at ESKOM there were corporate meetings underway to determine how the company could offer the cheapest electrical rates in the world over the next five years in order to stimulate economic development. ESKOM is a company with big visions and we might add, the talent to make them work. We met corporate leaders who were well educated and very knowledgeable about affairs in Africa and throughout the world. We also met highly qualified Blacks who were already in leadership positions and were being groomed for even more responsibility. We met computer experts, engineers, social workers, nurses and physicians who were the equal of any professionals of this type in the U.S. or Western Europe. Individuals in high management positions had training in economics or business administration and were making tough solid management decisions with a vision at least ten years down the road.

We were particularly struck by their confidence that they could solve difficult problems ranging from concerns of energy, ecology and community relations.

I found this collection of articles about EAPs in South Africa compiled by Paul Maiden, an excellent introduction to work related problems unfamiliar to North America. I believe that you will find this special edition as fascinating as I found South Africa to be.

Keith McClellan, Editor

Returning to Africa

South Africa is a country of great contrasts and controversy. It has been held up in the international spotlight and sanctioned for its policies of apartheid. Whether or not the sanctions have worked as intended is questionable and the subject of much debate. One can argue that the current changes underway in South Africa are more the result of international concern and internal pressure by those who have been subjugated under apartheid. It is a fair assumption that these combined forces have resulted in the tumultuous changes that have occurred in South Africa in the past few years.

Apartheid has been a sociological and psychological atrocity. It is going to take South Africa many decades to recover. Some rather heroic efforts are already underway as you will note as you read the articles in this edition. After several years of corresponding with EAP practitioners in South Africa this editor was presented with the unique opportunity to spend time in training and consultation in South Africa with a wide range of organizations. Invited by the Institute for Personnel Management to their annual EAP conference to present on evaluating the cost effectiveness of EAPs, the editor quickly realized that there have been significant developments in the EAP field in South Africa.

Being the first U.S. EAP practitioner to have the opportunity for first hand observation and examination of EAPs in South Africa the editor came to the realization that many of these professionals were toiling in relative obscurity due to international sanctions that frowned on any form of engagement or exchange. The decision to go to South Africa was not an easy one and was made with significant concern and trepidation relevant to my professional values, collegial relationships and what would be perceived as being "politically correct."

The final decision, however, emerged from none of these. Rather, it was based on a very personal decision to return something I had been given when I immigrated from Zimbabwe, Africa to the United States with my family in 1964 at the age of eleven. Through my interactions with numerous individuals from Zimbabwe and South Africa prior, during and subsequent to my visit there, I have become acutely aware of the advantages, opportunities and freedoms I was afforded in the United States thanks to the aspirations and vision of my parents Stanley and Elma Maiden. It is the goal of many immigrants seeking U.S. citizenship to become fully acculturated as quickly as possible and to become an "American" in every sense. I thought I had done that. I realize now that I never will. Although a naturalized American citizen, there remains a piece of "heart and soul" in Southern Africa. With that comes a personal commitment and responsibility to share what I have gained through my own "American experience" with my compatriots in Africa. More important, however, is the need to develop opportunities for dialog and an exchange of ideas which can only serve to educate and bring together. This special volume on EAPs in South Africa is intended for this purpose.

This volume may be considered controversial in the EAP field given the national origin of the contributing authors. I believe it will raise some questions but will provide some answers and will surely enlighten. I would like to thank Keith McClellan, Editor of *Employee Assistance Quarterly* and Bill Cohen, Publisher of The Haworth Press, Inc. for their encouragement and support of this special edition.

On a more personal note I would like to acknowledge Angela and Adrian du Plessis, Tracy and Rod Harper, Nana and Solly Moema, Claire and Rory Wilson, Ronel and Lourie Terblanche, Tertia and Chris Liebenberg, Rosemary and Mike Crouch, Glynnis and Lobby Russell, Ann and George Bennetts, Bernard Freeman, Sello Mkalipe, and Delphine Du-Toit – some of the "New South Africans" and proudly, some of my compatriots.

My Hope for a Bright Future for the Dark Continent

R. Paul Maiden
Chicago, Illinois

First World EAPs Serving Third World Clients: A U.S. Perspective of the South African Experience

R. Paul Maiden

SUMMARY. Employee assistance program models originating in the U.S. have been modified and incorporated in several countries. This article presents an overview of the development of EAPs in South Africa from the perspective of a U.S. EAP practitioner. The author has trained and consulted with EAP professionals in a range of industries in South Africa. This article is a retrospective of that experience.

South Africa is a country of paradoxes. Both beautiful and ugly, spirited and dispirited, intense and relaxed, homogeneous and heterogeneous, fearful and carefree. It is also a country that is undergoing rapid social change. All aspects of South African society are being affected and all are responding from their particular perspective. The goal of this social revo-

---

R. Paul Maiden is Chair, Occupational Social Work Program, University of Illinois at Chicago, Jane Addams College of Social Work and Research Associate, Jane Addams Center for Social Policy and Research. He is also the Consulting Director for Managed Care Services for Perspectives, Ltd., a Chicago-based EAP and managed mental health care firm.

The author wishes to thank members of the EAP Committee of the Institute for Personnel Management for making the visit to South Africa possible. He also wishes to thank the EAP representatives at Anglo American Corporation, Gold and Uranium Division, the Chamber of Mines, South Africa Synthetic Oils, Ltd. (SASOL), and Electric Supply Commission of South Africa (ESKOM) for their contributions to this article.

He may be contacted at the University of Illinois at Chicago, Jane Addams College of Social Work, Box 4348 (m/c 309), Chicago, IL 60680.

lution is the emergence of a "New South Africa"; the result of integrating and blending first and third world communities. There are many skeptics that discount the probability of this happening. A first hand view however, may change some minds. If not it would certainly lend a fresh perspective of the new found hope that is alive in so many black and white South Africans that want to put the atrocities of apartheid behind them and emerge as a respectable player on the world stage. This author has observed firsthand, some of the changes occurring in South Africa. More specifically, he has had the opportunity to consult with various employers and interview EAP professionals regarding the development of employee assistance programs in their respective companies. Further, he was presented the opportunity to examine the current development of EAPs throughout South Africa. This article is a retrospective of that experience with insight gained from the interaction with selected EAP professionals and treatment providers in South Africa.

EAP EVOLUTION IN SOUTH AFRICA

Employee assistance programs began to emerge in South Africa in the early 1980's. They are modeled after programs in the United States and were introduced to South African work organizations by social workers and psychologists who had studied programs in the United States. A number of individuals, it was also learned, have attended national EAPA and EASNA conferences and gleaned from them the "nuts and bolts" of EAP development and practice.

EAPs are a much younger field of practice in South Africa and thus do not have the rather colorful history that has accompanied the development of EAPs in the U.S. EAP practitioners in South Africa appear to be a more homogeneous group than EAP professionals in the U.S. South African EAPs are staffed predominantly by social workers, psychologists, nurses, medical officers, and labor relations personnel. This author did not come in contact with a single EAP practitioner who was a recovering alcoholic or substance abuser.

Because of the recent introduction of EAPs into South African work organizations they have essentially skipped a generation of development. This has both positive and negative implications. First, they have foregone the earlier controversies experienced by the field as it evolved from occupational alcoholism programs to employee assistance programs. For South African practitioners this has been positive in that it has enabled them to develop programs more rapidly. They have become conceptually more sophisticated in a much shorter period of time as they are a more professionally homogeneous group. They lack a core element however, which they could only have obtained from having experienced the growth of the field as we in the United States have. American EAPs are marked by their recognition that knowledge of addictions is a "core technology" of practicing in EAPs. The community of recovering EAP professionals has served as the "conceptual conscience" as the field has broadened its focus from alcoholism to the wide range of problems now encountered in EAPs. Alcoholism and drug addiction remain the most costly problems to an employer and thus require the most aggressive methods of intervention. South African EAPs address a similar range of clinical problems including addictions. It does not, however, appear to be a core technology. This was indicated in numerous interviews and informal conversations the author had with EAP professionals in South Africa who readily acknowledged that they possess minimal training and clinical expertise in the diagnosis, intervention and treatment of alcohol and drug abuse. This is not to suggest that they do not intervene with employees who have alcohol problems. They do. From their reports and the author's assessment, however, alcoholic and drug abusing employees who reach the EAP do so during the later stages of the disease when they have significant job performance and health problems that have resulted from an on-the-job accident or other major work related incident. At this point it has become obvious as to what the presenting problem is. The consequence is that South African EAP professionals have not practised early intervention as a means of more effectively dealing with employee substance abuse. The approach has been curative rather than preventative. It should be noted, however, as pointed out later in this article, the current sociopolitical environment of South Africa severely impacts the workplace and thus establishes a different set of priorities for EAP professionals. This has led to the development of EAPs that expend a vast amount of time and energy responding to employee problems that are wrought from a country whose most significant problem is that of apartheid (a legally mandated separation of the races).

A MACRO EAP MODEL

EAPs in South Africa stem from the same basic conceptual origins as EAPs in the United States. This is where the similarity ends. Employee assistance programs in South Africa have become the social conscience of the organizations in which they are ensconsed. In South Africa, the EAP is viewed by employees for the most part as an agent of change for social conditions in the work environment. The confidential nature of the EAP provides employees an avenue to discuss problems and air concerns that affect most employees. These problems differ somewhat from those presented by labor unions. Where the labor union bargains for working conditions, leave, pay, and the like, the EAP appears to assume the role of an ombudsman. The EAP presents to management issues regarding personal and/or family problems that affect a majority of the workforce resulting in significant human resource management problems for the employer (see du Plessis article in this volume).

One example is the development of the visiting wives program for miners. EAP counselors employed by Anglo American Corporation in the Gold and Uranium Division of the West Rand Region a short distance from Johannesburg, were successful in advocating on behalf of mine workers to arrange for two week in-resident visits by their wives.

Western Deep Levels is one of several mines operated by Anglo American, a multi-national and diversified corporation. Although the largest, it is one of several mining houses in South Africa. Western Deep Levels employs approximately 35,000 workers, 30,000 of whom live in large campus-like dormitories called hostels. Mine workers are recruited from African homelands and tribal regions where many have extended families and cultural ties. Miners do a nine month "tour of duty." At the end they are granted a 72 day leave. They must return at the end of the leave period at which time they re-enter the job that has been held for them. They also receive a pay raise. One of the problems that Anglo American experienced was the large number of miners who did not fulfill the nine month tenure. Many attempted to go home on weekends but due to distance and unreliable public transportation were tardy in reporting for their shift. Many others did not return at all. Employees were referred to the EAP for repeated tardiness and absenteeism or went to see a counselor on their own accord. Solly Moema and Chris Liebenberg, both EAP counselors at Anglo American, reported that employees complained of being homesick or were concerned about family matters such as aging parents, their children, finances, etc. Wives of some of the miners had also borne children in their absence. The counselors addressed this issue with management at Anglo American. The result was the development of the visiting wives quarters. Anglo American set aside land and built a group of small self-contained cottages. Employees could make application to have their wives come for a two week visit. During the stay miners moved from the hostel to the cottages. This gave the miners an opportunity to see their families between leave times and also was the time that miners and their wives discussed family matters and jointly made many of the decisions that concerned the family. Moema and Liebenberg reported that the program was so successful that Anglo American was planning on expanding the compound and building additional cottages.

Another example of an EAP that also deals with macro problems is the program at the Electric Supply Commission of South Africa (ESKOM). ESKOM provides ninety percent of electrical power to South Africa. It also provides services to Zimbabwe, Mozambique and Botswana. ESKOM maintains a training college equal in size to many college campuses complete with lecture halls and dormitories. Electrical workers from across Southern Africa are trained at the college in all aspects of electrical supply, from electrical engineering to maintenance work in power stations.

Chris Van Den Heever, Manager of Employee Well Being which includes the EAP, indicated that one of the major employee education efforts has been that of AIDS education. He reported that the number of AIDS cases found in the local workforce had been decreased due to intensive education. His impression was that the problem was more or less under control and that their workforce was educated in methods of preventing contraction of AIDS. A major concern was with workers who were coming to ESKOM for training. Most lived in rural areas and countries adjacent to South Africa where ESKOM provided services. ESKOM was in the process of determining whether or not to establish an AIDS testing program to screen HIV positive workers who would escalate the incidence of AIDS in the local population. Another avenue that was explored was developing an AIDS education program that ESKOM would take to the rural areas. Employees were educated at the work site but there was little or no education being conducted in the rural and remote areas. Employees were at the lowest risk of contracting AIDS while at their work stations. But the risk increased dramatically when they returned to their homes and communities.

The EAP counselors at Anglo American are even more aggressive in taking AIDS education to the community. In addition to the annual Health Expos where employees are educated regarding the risk factors in contracting AIDS, a Domestic Workers AIDS Education Program, a Youth Aids Education Program and a Hostel AIDS Induction Program were implemented. In the domestic workers program, a three day program was offered to individuals in local villages on AIDS and sexually transmitted diseases. The youth program provided sex education classes for teenagers at a municipal clinic and the local high school. Content on AIDS and other sexually transmitted diseases was included. In the hostel induction program, the EAP counselors include content on AIDS prevention while orienting new residents to the hostels. The annual Health Expos are the brainchild of the EAPs Regional AIDS Action Committee which covers several mines operated by Anglo Americans in South Africa. The Health Expo conducted pre- and post-surveys among hostel residents regarding awareness and attitudes towards AIDS. Referral and treatment procedures were also developed for HIV positive employees. Further, multi-lingual brochures were developed and distributed in all hostels. English and Afrikaans brochures were also sent to all homes in the region. A proposal was submitted for the installation of condom vending machines in each hostel. The EAP noted however, that the General Manager decided that distribution of free condoms would be more effective. AIDS education has become an integral element of South African EAPs given the prevalence of the disease throughout Africa.

Another project initiated by the EAP counselors was the implementation of a hostel arts and crafts project based on a needs analysis conducted by EAP counselors among hostel residents. Employees indicated a need for self-help skills in carpentry, bricklaying, shoe repairing, hairstyling, motor mechanics, tailoring, etc. Bricklaying was in the greatest demand and was offered at several mining sites. Participants in these projects were granted a certificate of competency after six months of training.

EAP counselors also implemented a Road Safety Awareness Project for employees due to a high rate of pedestrian and automobile accidents among workers. In response, the EAP initiated a prevention program aimed at reducing the accident rates. A Road Safety Awareness Day was planned. Some 3,000 workers engaged in competitions and simulations as a means of learning basic rules of road safety.

EAP counselors established an adult literacy program and enrolled employees and spouses in evening classes. A retirement project was also undertaken to address the needs and interests of retired employees and future retirees in an effort to establish short and long-term planning needs. Workshops on financial planning and other preparations for retirement were also conducted.

Another significant community project that the EAP counselors developed was a cross cultural awareness program. A recent annual report issued by the EAP at Anglo American stated that in light of the "harsh day-to-day challenges that face the co-existence of black and white employees social workers were prompted to launch a cross cultural program to promote better understanding of each other's backgrounds" (Anglo American, 1989). The program is initially targeted at the pre-school level with a long-term objective of expanding it to teenagers and parents. The program used a structured approach and interspersed constructive play and informal tutoring with mutual exposure to elementary English and Tswana, the dominant tribal language of the region.

The EAP also oversees a disabled rehabilitation program. In one region, an EAP counselor was responsible for rehabilitation efforts for 16 para and quadriplegic employees under sheltered employment as a result of mining accidents. The services center around development of self-supportive skills, and fitness and recreation activities. Disabled miners were trained in various aspects of commercial sewing as a method of becoming economically self-supportive. Once trained, they manufacture track suits. Disabled miners have the option of returning to their community or remaining at a hostel reserved for disabled miners.

These are just a sample of some of the macro activities that South African EAP counselors are engaged in. Many EAP counselors though, indicated serious concern for the lack of attention given to the individual clinical needs of employees. EAP professionals indicated that lack of a micro focus in their programs is a result of the demands for assistance with the vast social problems resulting from an apartheid society. They were unanimous in their recognition that there are a myriad of clinical needs that are going unmet or are only partially addressed due to the lack of treatment resources. Yet to be clarified and addressed are the effects of apartheid on the mental health of black and white South Africans alike. According to EAP professionals, macro practice will dominate EAPs and professionals will continue to deal with the symptoms of apartheid until a post apartheid South Africa emerges.

CURRENT CLINICAL ISSUES

South African EAPs follow a similar clinical model as EAPs in the United States. Counselors deal with a wide range of problems from alcohol and drug, marital, mental health and financial; most offer assessment and short term counseling but also may provide longer term intervention due to availability of community programs. In addition to clinical problems encountered in American EAPs, there are several problem areas that South African EAP counselors encounter that are quite disproportionate to their American counterparts. Two that are noteworthy are enuresis and sexually transmitted diseases.

The problem of enuresis appears to be restricted to black mining employees. According to J.C.C. Badenhorst, a clinical psychologist with the Chamber of Mines, "enuresis among the black adult male employees living in mine hostels is a phenomenon of concern for the individual, fellow residents, hostel management and EAP counselors'' (Badenhorst, 1990). A preliminary study on the phenomenon of enuresis among black mining employees found that alcohol abuse was a major contributing factor in the occurrence of bedwetting and was the most prominent and most closely associated with the magnitude of conduct and complaint incidents that were encountered among research subjects. Badenhorst indicated that the consumption of large quantities of traditional beer and the simultaneous effect of alcohol on sleeping patterns was evidenced. Traditional beer is a low alcohol beverage made from sorghum that is drunk primarily by black South Africans. It is readily available, quite cheap and is consumed in large quantities during one setting. Miners often drink at the company operated beer stalls after their shifts. Badenhorst also suggested that the possible effect of increased transient emotional stress among bedwetting employees warranted further investigation in lieu of one of his conclusions that ''the stress levels of bedwetting subjects may be affected by the risk to health and threat of death in deep level mining on the one hand and the specific stress of living in an isolated community away from family support systems for long periods of time on the other hand.'' As a result of this study, it was recommended that the EAP focus efforts towards assisting employees with the problem of enuresis. Bulletin boards now carry EAP posters offering help for this problem (see Badenhorst article in this volume).

A second very significant problem encountered by South African EAP programs is that of sexually transmitted diseases (STD) including AIDS, syphilis, and gonorrhea. One mine based EAP found that 22% of all EAP cases seen in 1989 were assessed with a STD. This was a trend that had continued from 1988. The development of massive employee and community education efforts was the response (Anglo American, 1990). EAP counselors indicated that AIDS is the single biggest health problem encountered by black South Africans. They also report that it is one of the most difficult problems about which to educate employees. AIDS has been politicized in South Africa and is viewed by more militant black South Africans as a scheme of the apartheid government to eradicate the black population. Prostitution is widely practiced in response to the many thousands of workers who live in single sex hostels. Many blacks also refuse to use condoms as they are viewed as the apartheid government's way of controlling the growth of the black population. One of the basic premises of black South Africa is that they will overpower the white dominated government and assume majority rule through sheer numbers. Thus, birth control is not practiced widely and many rural blacks are poorly educated in birth control methods. One can sense the frustration and futility that must be experienced by EAP professionals in dealing with this problem as it impacts the workplace.

Alcoholism and drug abuse cannot be discounted as they are also major problems encountered by EAPs. Counselors report that many mining accidents are the direct result of miners who are under the influence of mind altering substances. Alcohol is readily available and heavily abused. As mentioned above, workers living in hostels often spend their free time after work drinking to intoxication. Workers are isolated and there are limited outlets for other forms of recreation. Dagga (marijuana) is the leading drug of choice. Although illegal it is widely available and is considered potent. Counselors reported that miners often smoke prior to going down the mine shaft as it takes the edge off fatigue and fear.

TREATMENT RESOURCES

South Africa as a whole has very limited treatment resources for mental health and substance abuse problems. For black South Africans it is practically non-existent. Some mining companies and other large employers maintain their own hospitals some of which have facilities for the treatment of psychiatric and alcohol and drug problems. Psychiatrists are in short supply throughout South Africa and only number about 200. There are only three industrial psychiatrists, all of whom are employed by the Chamber of Mines, a prominent resource for mental health and substance abuse services of mine workers.

The Chamber of Mines of South Africa is a private enterprise service organization set up to promote and protect the interests of the South African Mining industry. It is a voluntary association of approximately 98 members which includes South Africa's six major mining finance houses, other mining companies and independent mines. The Chamber provides services to members that, among other things, include recruitment of some 500,000 workers from South Africa and other southern African countries through a network of 80 offices; negotiation of wages and conditions of employment with representatives of numerous trade unions; promotion of mine safety; coordination of member health care services; administration of hospitals serving the mining community; and provision of employee counseling and psychosocial services by the Chamber's employee assistance program (Chamber of Mines, 1989).

The Chamber offers a wide range of EAP services to employers. Some companies have no EAP and contract with the Chamber to provide the full scope of services. Anglo American for instance has a full service EAP. Counselors in this program provide assessment and in some instances short term counseling in addition to their other duties described previously. If an employee needs more intensive assistance he may be referred to the Chamber's EAP for longer term counseling or hospitalization. If an EAP counselor is unsure of assessment outcome he can consult with a psychologist or psychiatrist at the Chamber's EAP.

The Chamber is an example of a specialty EAP consortium that caters primarily to the mining industry. It has been one of the pioneers of EAPs in South Africa. Andre Beugger, Manager of EAP Services for the Chamber of Mines, indicated that one of their goals is to expand their services to employers outside the mining industry thus further developing the external model of employee assistance.

The South African National Council on Alcoholism (SANCA) is the second predominant provider of alcohol and drug abuse treatment. A nonprofit organization, SANCA maintains a number of clinics that provide education and treatment services to the mining community, other employer groups and the community at large.

A third avenue of treatment is available at a recently opened facility called Riverfield Lodge, the first private multi-racial treatment center in South Africa. Riverfield's parent company is Lifecare Clinics, Ltd., a 37 facility, 16,000 bed private health care group in South Africa. Lifecare covers a wide spectrum of health care, including medical and surgical services and long-term care of geriatric, psychiatric and infectious disease patients. Lifecare is generally recognized as an innovator in the health care field in South Africa. Riverfield Lodge is no exception. Located near Johannesburg, it is a 66 bed facility staffed by a full contingent of chemical dependency professionals and is similar in philosophy and treatment to any American chemical dependence treatment center.

CULTURAL AND ETHICAL ISSUES

Practicing under the social and economic conditions created by apartheid presents some daunting tasks for the EAP professional in South Africa. White South Africa is a first world country with all the benefits and accoutrements common to such prosperity. Black South Africa, on the other hand, is a third world country where conditions are exacerbated by the scourge of apartheid which is marked by the de jure and de facto policy that seals the fate of many blacks to lives of poverty, family separation, inferior education, disruption of community life, unsafe working conditions, and denial of basic essentials such as adequate food, shelter and health care.

Each is detrimental to the development, functioning and psychological well being of all the individuals that have been touched by this oppression and subjugation. It will take generations to eliminate the problems promulgated by apartheid South Africa. A post apartheid South Africa is sure to illuminate the extent of the psychological trauma to blacks and whites alike–something akin to post traumatic stress disorder of an entire society.

EAP counselors deal with these and many more issues in their day-to-day practice. Interviews with black and white EAP counselors revealed that they also encounter the same barriers in working with each other and that they must work to overcome them and understand each other's experiences and perspectives to enable them to work side by side as a group of professionals (see Moema and Thompson articles in this volume).

From a cultural perspective, EAP counselors must remain constantly aware of the ethnic variables presented by clients. Neither the black population or the white population are homogeneous groups. In one employee population there were nine ethnic groups represented. All were black but each may have different language dialects, tribal affiliations and religious beliefs. Tribal origin often dictates political affiliations which in turn frequently leads to intimidation between workers and violence between tribal factions. One method used in the mining industry to allow for language differentiation is the development of a single dialect. Fanakalo is drawn from each of the dialects and has been adopted as a common language among mine workers.

A cultural issue that EAP counselors and all mental health professionals must always remain cognizant of is the individual's belief in the healing powers of "muti" tribal or traditional medicine. Muti often consists of various concoctions of special herbs, barks and roots–and divination, a seeing into the past and future using bones (Mathabane, 1989). On one occasion the author was shopping in an open air market in Durban in Natal Province. Among the vendor stalls of fruits and vegetables, cosmetics, clothing, etc., was a vendor selling muti which consisted of an assortment of roots, herbs, fresh and dried animal entrails, monkey hands and bird heads.

Many workers seeking help from the EAP have also consulted their "nyanga" (medicine man) or "isangoma" (medicine woman). The nyanga or isangoma may recommend a remedy that may appear counterproductive to the EAP counselor's plan for treatment. The counselor cannot discount the muti of the nyanga or isangoma but must often times work in concert with them. To discount the power of muti to those who believe in it is to lose the confidence of the client. Furthermore, one never knows the positive effect the muti may have and whether success can be attributed to the power of suggestion or the natural healing power of the herbs, bark or roots that may have been prescribed by the tribal witch doctor. It is also noteworthy to mention that nyangas and isangomas are so widely used and respected that many insurance plans provide partial reimbursement for their services.

Another cultural peculiarity of many tribes is the belief in spirits. Interviews with counselors revealed that many EAP clients reported instances of "hearing voices in their heads." EAP assessments revealed the employee felt the need to get help because the "voices of their ancestors" had become bothersome and were disturbing their sleep thus causing fatigue and discomfort. Upon further inquiry, the EAP counselors revealed that many black ethnic groups believed that it was commonplace for the spirits of their ancestors to return and talk to them. It is only when they began to be "haunted" by them did they request help from the EAP and the full implications of their pathology emerged. The author was struck by the fact that by the time these individuals reached the EAP their mental illness was advanced to the point that they would disregard traditional folk ways in lieu of a contemporary solution. One wonders how many individuals must be in the early stages of such pathology and are getting no help.

There are also significant language and perceptual barriers experienced by black South Africans in describing symptomology. EAP counselors reported that there are no words in any African dialect for depression or alcoholism. Consequently, black clients who are depressed have difficulty describing what is wrong with them. EAP counselors indicated that they were able to diagnose depression when a black client reported that they "had a sadness that would not go away." Conversely, similar problems arise for counselors when they are dealing with alcoholism and its accompanying dynamics with a black client.

Issues of trust and confidentiality are also common to the EAP counselor and other mental health professionals. Steere and Dowall (1990) on writing about ethical dilemmas of clinical psychologists in South Africa suggest that effective intervention and treatment depends on a trusting relationship between client and therapist. This relationship is contaminated by the stereotyping and suspicion endemic to South Africa. Steere and Dowall note further that "by severely limiting social contact between blacks and whites, apartheid laws provide fertile ground for stereotyping. Uncertainty about the counselor's political stance is also likely to affect the establishment of trust." Therapists are supposed to remain value neutral to avoid influencing the client from accepting the counselors value systems. "Clients may however perceive 'neutrality' as threatening because of the political affiliations it might conceal." Steers and Dowall conclude that it is clear that without knowledge of such political stance clients may feel unable to talk openly, and many would not seek help.

MANAGED CARE IN SOUTH AFRICA

When questioned about managed care issues in South Africa, few EAP counselors had any knowledge or experience in this area. A recent article in the *South African Medical Journal* suggests that managed health care is on its way to South Africa. Broomberg, DeBeer and Price (1990) write that "there is strong evidence to suggest that managed care structures will generate significant savings and thus be more cost-effective than current private sector care." They also report that there are indications that large employers, as well as some of the large trade unions, are investigating and in some cases already negotiating the development of these structures. "This reflects the perception of the 'business community,' a large purchaser of private care, and that of the organized consumers of health care, that fee-for-service, 'third part payment' private health care is not cost effective and that significant improvements are possible" (Broomberg, DeBeer and Price, 1990). Consequently, private health care in South Africa will soon enter a period of substantial change.

TRAINING PROFESSIONALS

The growth in EAPs in South Africa has spurred the demand for training professionals for the field. A majority of EAP counselors interviewed held bachelors degrees. Some held masters degrees. There are few schools that offer occupational/EAP curriculum (see Mkalipe article in this volume).

Located in Johannesburg, the University of the Witwatersrand (commonly called Wits) offers an occupational specialization in its school of social work. "Wits" is internationally recognized for its anti-apartheid stance. Angela du Plessis, Director of the program, reported that the specialization started at the fourth year bachelors level, but is now a masters specialization. It should be noted the bachelors degree in South Africa has traditionally been a three year program with a fourth year being reserved for honor students. This model is giving way to the traditional four year program with a full contingent of graduate level courses. Du Plessis indicated that the occupational program at Wits has a definite macro focus in keeping with current demands of occupational practitioners. Clinical content appears to be minimized. Many EAP counselors viewed the program at Wits as being the pioneer in the formal training of workplace practitioners.

A second program is offered at Rand Afrikaans University (RAU) in Pretoria. Riaan Van Zyl, professor of social work at RAU, indicated that a masters clinical EAP specialization was recently developed. It was his impression, however, that an EAP training program with a clinical specialization was considered somewhat of an anomaly.

Professional development and continuing education for EAP professionals is offered through the Institute for Personnel Management (IPM). IPM is the equivalent of the American Society of Personnel Administration (ASPA). IPM established the National Employee Assistance Program Committee in April 1989. The EAP committee has elected officers representing numerous employers throughout South Africa. The group holds regular educational meetings and conducts an annual conference.

FUTURE PERSPECTIVES

The year of 1990 in South Africa was marked by dramatic social and political change. February, 1990 saw the unbanning of the African National Congress followed two weeks later by the release of Nelson Mandela. Pass laws were abolished and the Separate Amenities Act became an ugly footnote in history. This is only a beginning. February, 1991 marked another milestone in the dismantling of apartheid. President F. W. de Clerk announced his proposal to repeal the Group Areas and Land Act and eliminate the Population Registration Act, two laws that form the bedrock of grand apartheid. In June, 1991 these laws were repealed. There is much left to do before South Africa can take its place in the international community. The tasks that lie ahead are considerable. Prejudice and conflict will remain for decades to come. And, as demonstrated so often in many other societies, it will never be fully eradicated.

EAP professionals in South Africa have demonstrated remarkable achievements in the decade that there have been workplace intervention programs. Many of the first programs have been implemented in the mining industry. Their growth continues as other employers in South Africa begin to recognize the value of EAPs. They encounter barriers that most EAP professionals in the United States can hardly fathom. Their roles in work organizations are much more expansive than EAPs in American organizations. This occurred not out of design but out of demand from the employees and employers they serve. To date, their accomplishments are commendable. It will be interesting to observe their future progress, in the new South Africa.

REFERENCES

Anglo American Corporation of South Africa, LTD, Gold and Uranium Division, West Rand Region (1989). ''Annual Report of Social Services,'' Carltonsville, West Transvaal, South Africa.

Badenhorst, J.C.C. (1990). ''A Preliminary Study on the Phenomenon of Enuresis Among Black Mining Employees,'' Chamber of Mines of South Africa, EAP Services, Klerksdoup Centre for Human Development.

Broomberg, J., DeBeer, C. and Price, M.R. (1990). ''The Private Health Sector in South Africa–Current Trends and Future Developments,'' *South African Medical Journal*, Vol. 78(4), August, pp. 139-143.

Chamber of Mines of South Africa. (1990). ''The South African Mining Industry: Facts and Figures,'' Johannesburg, South Africa.

Mathabane, Mark (1987). *Kaffir Boy*, New York: MacMillan.

Steere, Jane and Terence Dowall (1990). ''On Being Ethical in Unethical Places: The Dilemmas of South African Clinical Psychologists,'' New York: Hasting Center Report, March/April, pp. 11-15.

The State of the Art of EAPs in South Africa: A Critical Analysis

Lourens S. Terblanche

SUMMARY. This article presents the findings from a study by which the author sought to determine the "state of the art" of EAPs in South Africa. The intent of the study was to determine the conceptual sophistication of EAPs currently operating in the South African business community. Standards used for the analysis are those developed by the leading occupational groups in the U.S.

Employee Assistance Programs in South Africa are a relatively new work place phenomena, despite assistance given to employees in the work place dating back at least four decades. However, EAPs are not managed and utilized to their fullest extent.

Assistance to troubled employees in the Republic of South Africa (RSA) is nothing new. However, the concept of "Employee Assistance Programs" (EAPs) in its traditional structured format, is quite new. This was demonstrated in a survey by this author, the research and findings of which will be discussed here.

BACKGROUND OF THE INITIAL STUDY

The survey was carried out by means of a questionnaire which was mailed to the respondents who were drawn from the membership of the Institute of Personnel Management of Southern Africa (IPM).

Lourens S. Terblanche, DSocSc (M.W.), is Senior Lecturer and Chairman of the Masters Program in Supervision at the Department of Social Work, University of Pretoria, Republic of South Africa. Terblanche currently serves as Chair of the National EAP Committee affiliated with the Institute for Personnel Management.

The questionnaire was compiled after completion of a literature review of the standards for an EAP compiled by the following American organizations: National Council on Alcoholism (NCA); Occupational Program Consultants Association; National Institute on Alcohol Abuse and Alcoholism (NIAAA); U.S. Office of Personnel Management (OPM); and the American Federation of Labor and Congress of Industrial Organizations (AFL-CIO).

The questionnaire was mailed to 600 members of the IPM–which was the total population of the specific category of membership. Membership requirements for this specific category were:

- registration as personnel practitioner with the South African Board for Personnel Practitioners;
- membership of at least three years with the IPM; and a minimum of four years of tertiary training with at least two years experience as a personnel practitioner.

There was a 16 percent response rate to the survey.

HISTORICAL DEVELOPMENT OF EAPs IN THE RSA

As mentioned previously, assistance to troubled employees in the South African workplace is well established. Structured assistance programs, however, have only developed since the early eighties. It would be impossible to sketch the historical development of EAPs in South Africa, without examining the development of occupational social work.

The first indication of assistance to employees in the industrial context was provided by the Chamber of Mines of South Africa. The COM is a coordinating body for the different mining houses and specifically had to deal with returning Second World War soldiers in the mid-forties. Many of these soldiers had no choice except to work on the mines–at that stage, more often than not, in the most undesirable conditions underground. Respiratory problems and lung disease were pervasive problems arising from these conditions. A hospital–Springkell Sanatorium–was erected at Modderfontein near Johannesburg to provide health care services to miners. This same facility has been utilized since 1961 for the treatment of miners with alcohol/drug problems and/or mental illnesses. It was initiated with the appointment of a social worker, who was primarily responsible for treatment of those miners who were more often than not chronically ill.

The South African Railways also contributed to the actual training of welfare officers since 1943 (Potgieter, 1970). ISCOR's (Iron and Steel

Corporation of South Africa) social work service was introduced in 1958 (Taute, 1975). Pieterse (1972) indicated that ISCOR already had ten social workers by 1969, compared with only four in 1960. SASOL, South Africa's foremost oil manufacturing company initiated its social work service in 1960 with the appointment of its first social worker.

The South African Defense Force (SADF) started its social work service in 1967 after an intensive investigation was launched into the conduct and behavior of national service men and permanent force members and the effect of family life on job performance (Alheit, 1972).

With reference to EAPs as such, a major development may be traced back to the beginning of the eighties. The Chamber of Mines of South Africa (COM) again initiated development when a consultant was appointed in 1983 to carry out a feasibility study on EAPs for the mining industry. This study represented a milestone in the historical development of EAPs in South Africa. In 1986 the concept was accepted in principle and the first two of seven counseling centers were introduced by the COM in two of the main mining areas in the country. This service currently consists of a professional staff exceeding a hundred people, of whom the majority have masters level training.

In 1983 a working group of EAPs was created under the auspices of the University of South Africa. In 1985, this working group was incorporated into the membership of the Institute for Personnel Management of Southern Africa (IPM). The working group, known as the National EAP Committee, elected officers in 1989 during a national seminar and represents some of the main industries, two universities and a social service agency.

SURVEY RESULTS

Nature and Description of EAPs in South Africa

It was learned that only 69 percent of respondents actually offered assistance to their employees. Of those 69 percent, only 58 percent offered assistance according to a structured program, while the balance offered services in an unstructured way, which cannot be described as an EAP.

EAP Models

An EAP needs to be introduced according to a specific model to meet the specific needs and demands of a specific organization. An ideal and suitable model could contribute to the enhancement of an effective service to employees.

As described in Table 1, the majority of employers responding have developed in-house model EAPs, or a combination thereof. Also significant was the fact that a large percentage (37.5 percent) did not or could not describe the model implemented in their company.

Race as a Factor in Access to EAPs

In view of the traditional distinction and discrimination between race groups, data were obtained on the accessibility of services to all race groups. It was learned that 89 percent of employers offered their services to all race groups. Nine percent gave no indication of their approach while only two percent discriminated according to race. According to data obtained regarding services to employees, it is noted that race as such does not play a role in the accessibility of services to various employees where there is a properly conceptualized EAP.

A review of the literature suggests that employers that implement EAPs as an employee benefit tend to be some of the most racially progressive and rank high in terms of corporate social responsibility. It is no surprise, therefore, that the respondent companies have EAPs and thus would be expected to some degree to be more racially conscious regarding EAP access to all employees.

Policy on EAPs

The policy statement is a crucial component of an EAP, which provides the opportunity to stipulate specifics with regard to those aspects that need

TABLE 1

MODELS OF EAPS

Model (N=64)	Number	Percent
In-house	22	34
External/contract	10	16
Consortium	02	03
Union based	01	1.5
Combined: In-house/external	05	08
No indication	24	37.5
TOTAL	64	100

to be addressed. Table 2 indicates that a small majority of employers (53 percent) do provide assistance according to a formal policy, and that this same small majority (55 percent) stressed the importance of confidential handling of information in the policy statement.

A majority of responding employers (48 percent) do provide particulars on the procedure to be carried out by supervisors in case of mandatory referrals, while only 14 percent do not provide particulars on the referral procedure.

Further, half of the responding employers (50 percent) do provide particulars on the procedure for voluntary referrals. In comparison with the findings in the previous paragraph, a balanced focus on voluntary referrals was confirmed.

Involvement of Management, Supervisors, and Labor Force

Involvement of management, supervisors and the total labor force is necessary for the successful functioning of an EAP. With reference to the involvement of management, supervisors and the labor force itself, the following results were obtained.

Participation of management was confirmed by 58 percent, while lack of participation was confirmed by 33 percent. The balance of nine percent was made up of respondents who did not give a response to the specific question or whose response was unusable.

With reference to participation of the labor force in designing and implementing a program, the study found that only 25 percent provided for input from the labor force. The majority (66 percent) of respondents

TABLE 2

POLICY ON EAP'S

N=64	Percentage			
	Yes	No	N/A	No Indication
Formal policy	53	47	--	--
Maintenance of confidentiality	55	3	31	11
Procedure: mandatory referral	48	14	30	8
Procedure: voluntary referral	50	25	16	9

confirmed no input by employees. Three percent indicated that the question was not applicable to their situation, while six percent did not answer the question.

Involvement of management in an EAP in South African organizations is quite strong. Participation of the labor force is limited and does need attention, which could be dealt with by means of orientation of management and the labor force itself.

Physical Location of EAPs

The physical location of the offices of the EAP personnel determines to a great extent the degree of support for the program. Location should enhance participation in the program by means of the assurance that confidentiality will be respected. As noted by Myers (1984):

> The counseling office site can undo the best efforts to retain client confidentiality. Employees simply are not going to refer themselves to a counseling office if there is a chance they will be seen in the office or upon entering or leaving it.

Seventy-eight percent of respondents confirmed the importance of convenient accessibility of EAP offices, while 11 percent held a contradictory opinion. Six percent viewed the question as inappropriate to their situation and three percent did not provide an answer. Two percent of the responses were unusable.

Record Keeping Systems

Record keeping is sometimes seen as being of minor importance. The opposite to this viewpoint is, however, true as a confidential recording system is viewed as critical to the success of an EAP.

In this study, 50 percent of respondents confirmed the existence of a separate file for EAP records while 28 percent indicated that clinical EAP records were kept in the general personnel file. Nine percent indicated that EAP records are filed in both the personnel and a separate clinical file. Six percent of respondents gave no response, while five percent indicated that records were not maintained at all. Two percent viewed the question as inappropriate to their situation.

These findings indicate that approximately half of employers surveyed were generally insensitive to the need to maintain separate clinical records. This correlates with an earlier finding that only 55 percent of policy statements address confidentiality as integral to the EAP. Lack of confidentiality as an integral issue in the operation of the EAP was also demonstrated by the finding that access to records limited to the EAP staff accounted for only 33 percent of the employers surveyed. Thus, in the majority of the companies, personnel other than EAP staff could access the file at will.

Insurance Coverage for Treatment

Health insurance coverage for treatment of psycho-social problems can contribute significantly to the motivation of a troubled employee when in the process of deciding on treatment for his/her problem. Financial difficulties very often go hand-in-hand with the existence of social problems. Health insurance coverage for alcohol, drug, and mental health problems is sporadic in South Africa. Table 3 presents types of coverage available among employees surveyed.

One respondent confirmed that the employer himself took responsibility for the treatment of alcoholism and drugs (no coverage by their medical insurance). One respondent confirmed that the entire treatment was free, as a consortium was covering the costs. Psychological and psychiatric treatment are covered by most medical plans (84 percent and 81 percent, respectively). Coverage for treatment of alcoholism was confirmed by 56

TABLE 3

COVERAGE OF COSTS BY MEDICAL FUNDS

Type of Problem (N=64)	Number	Percent
Psychiatric and psychological treatment	18	28
Alcoholism, drugs, psychiatric, psychological	17	27
Alcoholism, drugs, psychiatric, psychological, marital	11	17
Alcoholism, psychiatric and psychological	5	8
Alcoholism and drug	1	1.5
Alcoholism and psychological treatment	1	1.5
Alcoholism, drugs and psychological	1	1.5
Psychiatric, psychological treatment and marital problems	1	1.5
No indication	5	8
No coverage of costs at all	4	6
TOTAL	64	100

percent. Only six percent confirmed that their employee health plan did not cover any chemical dependency or mental health problems.

EAP Steering Committees

Historically, the existence of an EAP Steering Committee has and continues to be of major importance in the functioning of an EAP. This survey found that 63 percent of respondents have no allowance in their EAP for a steering committee. Thirty percent confirmed the existence of such a committee which accepts co-responsibility for the management of the program. Only six percent of those 30 percent did provide for representation on the steering committee by the labor force itself. When considering the important role played by the steering committees, this finding suggests a significant shortcoming in the operation of South African EAPs.

EAP Staffing

With reference to the composition of EAP staff, information was gained on the various professions involved in the EAP field as this could be a contributing factor to the successful functioning of an EAP. It was learned that the majority of programs (58 percent) are staffed by personnel practitioners; nursing staff (44 percent) and medical officers (39 percent) are the second and third largest professional groups to be represented as EAP staff. Social workers are utilized by 33 percent of programs.

The majority of programs are staffed by personnel officers, which could have resulted from the fact that EAPs were merely added to the existing tasks of staff already responsible for other tasks. The reality of medical officers and nursing staff being active in industry for a long period of time could also be an explanation for the large number of programs making use of those professionals. The phenomenon of social workers being the fourth largest professional group to be utilized by EAPs could be an indication of the fact that social workers have not yet been settled and accepted in industry as well as one would have expected.

Marketing Techniques

Marketing of EAPs plays an important role in the development and acceptance of EAPs in industry.

Although there are a variety of marketing techniques (see Table 4), only a few are applied quite commonly. Orientation courses are utilized by 69 percent of programs to do marketing for EAPs; posters are utilized by 34 percent, while newsletters are utilized by 28 percent and 27 percent

TABLE 4

MARKETING TECHNIQUES

Technique	Percent
Induction and orientation courses	69
Posters	34
Newsletter (once)	28
Newsletter (regular)	27
Introductory meeting	27
Letters to family members (once)	13
Notice clipped to salary slips	11
Personal notification after identification	06
Personal interviews	03
Letters to family members (regular)	03
Training of supervisors	03
Meeting with representatives of the labor force	1.5
Information at normal scheduled meetings	1.5
Videos	1.5
Employer guide	1.5
Managerial training	1.5
Lifestyle programs	1.5
Information in internal telephone directory	1.5
Regular interviews with human resources department	1.5
Marketing still in process if development	1.5
Informal marketing (?)	1.5
No marketing carried out	08
Provide no indication	03
Not applicable	06

respectively for a single and repeated marketing attempt; special marketing meetings are applied by 27 percent of employers surveyed; and eight percent of respondents undertake no marketing at all.

Management/Union Training

Training managers and union representatives is vital to achieve an understanding of not only the mere existence but also of the influence of social problems on productivity. The researcher has tried to ascertain to what extent such information was provided to the different categories of people in industry. Table 5 presents a breakdown of this data.

When the different categories are compared, it appears that management is best informed on the existence of social problems (69 percent). Supervisors are the second best informed category (56 percent), while

TABLE 5

INFORMATION TO STAFF ON SOCIAL PROBLEMS

Category of Staff N=64	Percentage			
	Yes	No	N/A	No Indication
Management	69	22	-	09
Supervisors	56	33	-	11
Union representatives	19	69	03	09

union representatives are trained in only 19 percent of the programs. When the key role of the supervisor in the actual functioning of the EAP is taken into consideration, it is of great concern that only 56 percent of the programs are actively engaged in training supervisors. The lack of training to union personnel is of equal concern.

Treatment and Community Resources

To manage an EAP successfully, it is necessary to have access to a wide range of resources, given that EAP staff very often lack the competency to fulfill the different roles, especially the role of therapist. Information was obtained on the existence of community resource guides and the evaluation of the actual services provided by those resources.

Fifty eight percent of programs had developed a listing of community resources; 33 percent had no referral resources; one percent viewed the question as inappropriate to their circumstances and eight percent did not respond to the question. Forty-two percent confirmed evaluation of services prior to utilizing those resources; 6 percent confirmed no evaluation; eight percent did not give an indication, while 34 percent viewed the question as inappropriate to their unique circumstances. This finding suggests a deficit in available resources and in some instances, failure on the part of the EAP counselor to maximize development and utilization of available resources.

Evaluation and Cost-Effectiveness of EAPs

The development of EAPs is typically based on humanitarian or economic agendas or a combination thereof. Being able to identify which agenda is primary and which is secondary will dictate the strategy used to market EAP implementation to employees.

The survey found that only 1.5 percent of respondents had a pure economic motive for the introduction of an EAP; 41 percent had a purely humanitarian motive when introducing their EAP; 9.5 percent did not give an indication, and three percent viewed the question as inappropriate to their situation.

Sixty-two percent of respondents confirmed the importance of the EAP to demonstrate cost-effectiveness; 19 percent viewed proof of cost-effectiveness to be not important and 19 percent did not give an indication of their specific views on this matter.

The respondents confirmed the existence of a strong humanitarian motive for the introduction of an EAP. Consequently, motive would also have an influence on the importance of evaluating and determining the cost-effectiveness of programs. Although humanitarian motives play a stronger role than economics in South African EAPs, there is still concern among employers about the cost-effectiveness of their EAPs, as such.

Educating Employers About EAPs

To a great extent, this was an exploratory study due to the absence of similar studies in the South African context. Consequently the need for information among South African employers was examined.

Seventy-two percent of those organizations already providing an EAP confirmed a need for information on the subject, while 52 percent of those not providing an EAP voiced a need for information. This response suggests a high degree of need for information on EAPs, as strongly confirmed by the uncertainty among South African employers regarding the nature and value of EAPs. It did, however, confirm a sensitivity to the potential value and possible contribution of EAPs to work organizations.

CONCLUSIONS AND RECOMMENDATIONS ON EAPs IN SOUTH AFRICA

The most significant finding from this study is that EAPs in South Africa are just beyond their infancy but still are not utilized to their fullest potential. This study also suggests that EAPs in South Africa are somewhat rudimentary. Although they have been established within the conceptual parameters as intended, they lack operational specifics, e.g., comprehensive training for managers and union personnel, development of more sophisticated record keeping procedures to ensure limited access and enhanced confidentiality, and staffing of the EAP by personnel with substance abuse and mental health expertise. EAPs in South Africa can be enhanced by means of the proper development of training activities (supervisory training, but even more important, training of EAP professionals), marketing and evaluation skills. South African EAPs have demonstrated remarkable growth in their short life span since introduction to the South African workplace. They also present a significant opportunity for employees and a challenge to employers and professionals alike.

REFERENCES

Alheit, H.K.J. (1972). Suid-Afrikaanse Militere Welsynsdiens. *Volkswelsyn En Pensioene*, 7(2), 29-33.

Myers, D.W. (1984). *Establishing and Building Employee Assistance Programs*, Connecticut: Quorum Books.

Pieterse, F.P. (Dec. 1972). Aspects of professional manpower in social work. *Social Welfare and Pensions*, 7(2), 19-23.

Potgieter, M.C. (1970). *Maatskaplike Sorg in Suid-Afrika.* RGN Publikasie. Reeks No. 43. Stellenbosch: Universiteitsuitgewers.

Taute, M.P. (1975). Bedryfsmaatskaplike Werk Binne Die Opset Van 'n Swaar Nywerheid. *Volkswelsyn En Pensioene*, 10(2), 27-31.

EAPs in South Africa: A Macro Model

Angela du Plessis

SUMMARY. EAPs in South Africa are best characterized as macro model as opposed to the U.S. micro model EAP. Although EAPs in South Africa were initially modeled after U.S. programs, they have evolved into something quite different. This article examines the rationale for the evolution of the macro model EAP in South Africa in light of the country's socio-political, economic and racial problems.

The assumption underlying this article is that it is both desirable and natural that EAPs evolve, over time, to embrace macro practice. Micro practice is understood largely as one-to-one or one-to-family clinical counseling or casework the focus of which is a personal problem orientation, or an emphasis on the "employee-as-person." Macro practice, on the other hand, includes collective and organizational problems which have a workplace and/or systemic orientation–a focus on the "person-as-employee." Of course some problems may have aspects of both. It is not the contention of the writer that micro practice be abandoned; rather that good EAP practice will include both micro and macro practice.

The argument is not necessarily that EAP practitioners become organization development specialists immediately, viewing themselves as the panacea for every organizational problem. However, Googins (1986) has pointed to the problem of "EAP foreclosure." By this he means the limi-

---

Angela du Plessis, MSc (Oxford University), is Director of the Industrial Social Work Program at the University of the Witwatersrand in Johannesburg, South Africa. She is completing a PhD in Industrial Social Work from the University of the Witwatersrand and has consulted extensively with companies throughout South Africa.

tations arising from EAPs based on the psychiatric/medical model which tends to highlight individual causation in problem aetiology. This can lead to efforts aimed at changing the person, with a concomitant lack of attention to environmental and systemic stressors. Such an approach may result in misdiagnosis of problems, ineffective intervention and the EAP remaining on the periphery of the organization.

It is interesting to contrast this approach with that of Kurzman and Akabas (1981), two pioneers in occupational social work, although their argument does not necessarily contradict the ideas in this article. They believe that excellence in occupational social work practice is achieved by sticking to the "core competencies" and "authenticity" of social work. This they see as seeking out and dealing with people problems. Indeed, the clinical/counseling set of skills is often what defines the "specialness" of social work input at the workplace. They believe that social workers should only move onto "indirect" macro tasks such as consultation to management once they have earned this evolvement through people oriented intervention. It would thus be from a solid practice base that social workers move to macro services.

Nevertheless, evolvement in services from micro to macro practice is inherent in basic social work theory. The current metaphor here is the ecological model which views man always in relation to his environment or context. It is within the interactions between man and his environment that problems occur. Environmental change is therefore an important element in practice interventions. The three main social work methods–casework, groupwork and community work–beg that the social worker look upstream from the individual to broader social units and systems. The workplace is an excellent example of a functional/geographic community which impacts directly on individuals and groups, with a great deal of opportunity for community work with task, process and relationship goals. Finally, inherent in good social work practice should be a move away from tertiary to primary prevention. Such a commitment demands a repertoire of practice skills that goes beyond personal counseling on an individual or micro level. When we talk about evolvement from micro to macro practice we are talking about two related aspects. The first is the way we diagnose problem causation and the second is the way we plan to intervene. Thus there are both ideological/philosophical implications as well as practical/logistical implications of one's micro/macro frame of reference.

There are some special circumstances in the South African workplace which highlight even more the need to have a "macro" perspective. These relate to systemic and environmental issues which impact on workers and thus come to the attention of the EAP practitioner. Problems here include those rooted in socio-political circumstances beyond the control of individual workers. One example is the migrant labor system which gave rise to the single sex hostels found in the mining industry. Alcohol abuse is a common problem in these hostels. A micro approach–offering, say, counseling to individual employees–will only ever have limited impact. Issues which need to be addressed include employee housing schemes, systems governing hostel life, safety in the workplace, recreation and patterns of family visits.

An example of a problem begging a more macro approach is violence in the townships and the company's response to it. Many problems brought to the EAP by black workers have their roots in racial discrimination and lack of cross-cultural awareness and contact. Micro-oriented individuals working to deal with collective and systemic issues may not be appropriate. However, problems found universally in workplaces may require a more macro approach if one is alert to the way the work process, nature of work, and organization of work impact on individuals and groups of workers. Examples are the effects of shift work and the effects of spending many hours traveling to and from the workplace. The latter is a major problem in South Africa where townships are often in isolated areas. Work accidents, workplace violence, and aspects of safety are also examples. Organizational policies, procedures and culture impact on workers as well. One female single parent with a financial problem may highlight an anachronistic policy inconsistently which allows only men to obtain housing loans from the company.

With their emphasis on the "troubled employee" EAPs grounded in the medical/psychiatric model may cause practitioners to miss the "troubled department." Or indeed, the "troubled organization." On analyzing her counseling statistics, one local social worker noted a high number of referrals from one department. On investigation it was found that this department was the only one to work a 24 hour shift and have strict deadlines. In such cases, individuals may not require intervention; instead the following may be appropriate targets for change: patterns of reward, communication styles, discriminatory workplace practices, unrealistic production expectations, safety policies and unfair personnel practices.

In an article written in 1984, Winkelpleck (1986) looks at the directions EAPs are taking highlighting evolvement towards organizational methods. Winkelpleck introduces into the concept of the "organization as client," pointing out that in many cases, "The EAP is, in reality, an organizational assistance program." Winkelpleck argues that individuals cannot be dealt with without looking at the entire organization in which they function–an ecological perspective. Winkelpleck asserts that organizational development is a legitimate function of the EAP. She describes this function as involving "an assessment of how the organization could be 'treated' to heal itself." She states that:

> EAP staff are in a unique position to encourage organizational development (OD). EAP staff have the greatest access to the widest variety of employees in the least authoritarian manner of anyone in the entire organization. EAP staff, especially in-house, speak to all levels of employees and, thus, develop a view of the organization as a social system. While organizational administrators are ultimately the decision-makers and movers of OD ideas, EAPs can serve to analyze the organization and propose specific development ideas.

Examples of ideas given are post trauma intervention and introducing new employees to the organization utilizing time-limited, cross-department support groups.

Ford et al. (1985) address organizational wellness, which they describe as a new slant for EAPs. The writers purport that "there are several signs of organizational dysfunction that EAPs are in a unique position to detect . . . taking an OD perspective can increase the constructive options available to the EAP in such contexts." However, as is pointed out by the writers, OD has often been avoided by both management and unions–by management because of fear that OD will lead to adversarial conflicts and rebellion and by unions because of an association of OD with the time and motion efficiency programs for the 1930s. Ford et al., call for EAPs to "incorporate approaches to OD which promote organizational wellness hand in hand with employee wellness." In their article, the writers give five primary interfaces between the EAP and the organization which provide entry points for EAP-based OD since they can highlight organizational problems.

These are counseling and referral of employees, referral-oriented consultation with supervisors, managers and union officials as well as the submission of EAP reports. Examples of OD interventions arising from traditional EAP functions provided practitioners have a macro perspective are given. One relates to a sergeant in the police department who refers an officer without initially confronting that person because he thinks "the officer works well only if given complete free reign." In the words of Ford et al., "discussion with the sergeant revealed that other police supervisors feel a similar conflict between direct and laissez-faire leadership. They are uncertain about how to best mould a cohesive work team with their 'lone ranger' officers. Discussion of this issue with the police chief sparks his decision to bring in an OD consultant who can conduct leadership, stress management and team building workshops." This example illustrates the contention that the EAP can serve as an OD catalyst. The meeting of the core mission of the EAP–to enhance employees' resources for self improvement–is facilitated by this OD perspective.

Santa-Barbara and Coshan (1988) also write about "the workplace as a source of stress." They report that 25-30% of employees they see as EAP service providers have work-related problems which contribute to their distress. If one has only a "micro" perspective, such problems may be misdiagnosed or lead to superficial treatment of symptoms. What is needed is competent assessment of workplace (environmental) stressors. Santa-Barbara and Coshan identify three categories of work stressors: informal aspects of the workplace, pseudoformal stressors and formal aspects of the workplace. The intervention for workplace stressors may only seldom be individually-based. Here, EAP providers may have to play roles in management consulting, job design and organizational effectiveness.

In all writings dealing with evolvement of EAP intervention from micro to macro or individual to the organization, the central issue of sanction is mentioned. Of course broader intervention would require the sanction of management–but also the sanction of employees who may feel confidentiality will be compromised should their grievances be known. Such issues must be addressed in the process of making private troubles public issues and of making individual problems collective ones.

TWO MODELS: MICRO TO MACRO

There are a few "models" showing the evolvement of occupational social work from micro to macro intervention (Frank & Streeter, 1985). Two will be presented here. The first model comes from Ozawa (1980) and consists of four "stages" of practice.

Model One

Stage 1: Single Service Orientation

Here, social services are organized around one or two specific problems. Examples could be alcohol abuse or AIDS. The focus is often on the "employee-as-person."

Stage 2: Comprehensive Services

More comprehensive services may be developed as it becomes recognized that problems dealt with in Stage 1 are symptoms of underlying concerns. Thus intervention is broadened to embrace educational programs and consultation with management. Although the use of the group as an intervention strategy may be adopted, the orientation, as Ozawa points out, remains towards the individual as the unit of need.

Stage 3: Organizational Intervention

Here, a focus on the "person-as-employee" is introduced. In the words of Ozawa, attention is given to the human relations and motivational needs of workers. Results of interventions may be job reorganization and adaptation in relationships between workers. Changes in production lines, work groups and job design are examples as well. Ozawa notes that a primary limitation is that intervention would have to be management sanctioned and thus would probably only happen if it appears cost effective and has a positive impact on productivity.

Stage 4: Community Building

Here, common objectives of employees and management are emphasized. Intervention is represented by social services which promote a sense of "community" in the workplace. Thus community development skills would be used to enhance employer participation and decision-making.

According to Ozawa, each stage represents:

a. a development in the knowledge and skills base of the social worker
b. a developing value orientation
c. an evolvement in the level of change which may be obtained (micro to macro)

Each stage also represents potential for further integration of the social work function into the organization–from a fairly peripheral role to one much more enmeshed with organizational dynamics, power and resources.

The second "model" traces the development of occupational social work (Googins, 1987). Googins writes that "the more occupational social work takes root and matures, the more complex becomes the practice." He further outlines 5 stages:

Model Two

Stage 1: Welfare Capitalism

This period has been viewed as representing the roots of occupational social work. Paternalism and anti-union sentiments abounded. Basic employee needs covering a wide spectrum were addressed.

Stage 2: Personal Problem Orientation

Here the individual was at the center of activities. This reflected the predominant casework orientation of social work and focused primarily on alcoholism in the workplace. There was only some conceptual acknowledgment of any larger context. Employee assistance programs were the major vehicle for service delivery.

Stage 3: Service Model

The major development in this stage is giving attention to systemic problems. Organizational problems are addressed, which represents a marked ideological shift and could result in conflict between occupational social workers and EAP practitioners who expounded a narrower focus. Influenced by the ecological model and systems theory, analysis of problem causation extends beyond the individual to incorporate the context–both the organization and the larger environment. Programs do not get defined from a particular problem, but adapt to changing needs of employees and their environment, thus creating a *service* model, responsive to a broad range of dynamic employees' needs. Both the concepts of client and service expanded beyond traditional counseling. Proactive interventions are encouraged; for example, easing the stress of lay-offs; needs assessments; retirement seminars and responding to those problems generated within the workplace. Googins does point out that this step has been controversial. Some argued it would "dilute the focus on alcohol, get away from a core technology, become a mental health program or in general become all things to all people and therefore discredited or extinct" (p. 42).

Stage 4: Prevention Model

Stages 2 and 3 rely on tertiary prevention. In Stage 4 the focus changes once again to prevention programs with the primary goal of improving and maintaining employee health. Although the client system shares the broad focus of Stage 3 (that is, potentially all employees, not only those with a particular problem) the new orientation is, towards including "low risk, non-problem populations" (p. 43). Googins cites Martin Shain's definition of health promotion programs as a "wide gamut of interventions, having as their common denominator the intention to mobilize the self-regulatory drive of individuals and groups to govern their own health and wellbeing" (p. 43).

Thus, education programs are used to encourage employees to take responsibility for their own health and wellbeing. Googins asserts that this "represents a major cultural and organizational shift for more organizations since it links corporate goals directly with the preservation and maintenance of healthy employees and the environment. The new direction assumes shared roles and responsibilities with families and communities for achieving desired goals of healthy and productive employees, families, communities and work organizations" (p. 44).

Googins comments that this approach is compatible with social work's theory and mission since it spans the range of prevention from primary through secondary to tertiary. Googins, however, writes that this stage is still exploratory for three reasons. First, there are few studies which have linked prevention with increased productivity and therefore its cost-effectiveness is not as easy to demonstrate as it may be in the case of EAPs. Second, the organizational "home" of such programs is unclear. It may be an extension of the EAP, attached to the medical department or be autonomous. Third, practitioners themselves have not moved to this stage. Dilemmas are faced at each progression and some would argue that the new roles go beyond the expertise, training and education of EAP practitioners, thus making it difficult to enter this stage.

Stage 5: Organizational Change

Googins does highlight that there is no "real model" in practice, but that this stage "represents an idiosyncratic set of activities in which a small number of occupational social workers have been engaged" (p. 45). On a trip to Europe, Googins did find this stage more developed there, especially in Holland (Googins et al., 1986).

Another limiting factor Googins emphasizes is the degree of credibility occupational social work has to achieve before entering this stage of program maturity. One of the major tasks is to "balance clinical and individual needs with environmental and organizational factors contributing directly or indirectly to the individual's problem" (p. 45). What is central to underpin evolvement is the degree of *integration* of the social work function within the organization.

The issue of integration is elaborated upon by Googins et al. (1986) in an excellent article in which they compare occupational social work in America and Europe. Integration into the organization can be both a precondition for and a result of macro practice. Googins et al. define "integration" as the linking of the occupational social work function with the needs, goals and values of the work organization. Googins and his colleagues noticed that "integrated" programs in Europe had at least three common elements: first, knowledge and understanding of the social work program was universal; second, the program was utilized by the company for more than individual problems; third, the agenda of the social worker was proactive and organization-wide.

Googins et al. outlines three factors which contribute to integration.

1. The degree of integration is a developmental process–the maturing process of occupational social work is a broadening process by which the needs of the organization and the expertise of the social workers and their programs become better known and are drawn upon.
2. The process of integration has to be purposeful–if integration into the mainstream is to occur, a purposeful strategy and plan need to be adopted. The proactive position conceptualizes the client to be the organization, its needs to exist on macro and micro levels, with the social worker playing a critical role in identifying, analyzing and working with the organization around the solution to the problem. Unless this broad conceptualization of the client system is held, and a purposeful strategy is developed, the social worker will tend to relate to a narrow (although important) function and risk being tangential to the organization.
3. The process of becoming integrated is essentially political–all organizational players compete for scarce resources, vie for influence and power and seek to secure their positions and value to the organization. If social workers desire to move towards the core of the organization and become valued and integrated . . . they cannot be exempt from these dynamics and in fact have to master them if they wish to achieve their goals. Integration comes through acceptance and fighting through turf battles, power struggles, organizational alliances and status issues. All of this requires a real political savvy which can plot out a path, build alliances and gain the credibility needed to achieve the goal of integration.

In an excellent article written over a decade ago, Steiner and Borst (1980) advocate for an expanded role for American social workers in industrial settings. They point out that the service motif of increasing systemic restorative and preventive services is underdeveloped in the United States where social workers have limited themselves to a clinical practice orientation.

An example of expanded practice was given from the Dutch Steel Industry. Key performance areas for social workers were as follows:

a. Giving aid to individual employees who have social problems which affect their wellbeing at work.
b. Giving aid to functional groups within the company where relationship problems occur.
c. Paying particular attention/care to vulnerable groups of employees, including migrants, aging employees and employees with limited job openings.
d. Participating in the support of social-organizational processes in the workplace such as reorganization.
e. Helping to detect social-structural problems and contributing to their solution from a welfare point of view.
f. Helping to keep track of social developments and their impact on the industrial community in order to investigate their implications for the company.

Such an integrated, macro approach (which includes micro practice) was facilitated by the employment of a new director of social work who had expertise in working with systemic change within a preventive orientation. He created the expectation, and then responded to it, that problematic working conditions can be reduced while the productivity of the industry be maintained or improved. He supported employee participation as an essential ingredient in efforts to reduce problematic working conditions. He demanded and received assurance that social work was recognized as a profession and that the actions of social workers would have some independence from administrative structures, whether these structures be management or labor. In disputes concerning social work actions, the social work Code of Ethics was to be the final authority. He also required that the social work department have responsibility for setting policy regarding client records and that confidentiality of employees contacted be respected. He also developed ongoing training programs for social workers, rewarded those who showed professional development, developed more job security and obtained commitment to improving the social worker-employee ratio. The projected target was 1:1500. Another factor assisting the expanded role was the important decision to decentralize the service so that social workers' offices were on-site. All of the above illustrates principles of good occupational social work practice and set the framework for an expanded role.

This article is not meant to detract from micro, individual practice. There will, and must, always be a place for this in EAPs. However, micro practice is only part of the total picture and should be viewed as such.

In an unpublished paper entitled "The Organization as Client: Broadening the Concept of EAPs," Googins and Davidson (1989) outline the opportunities and risks of broadening the EAP client system to include the organization and community. Opportunities are:

a. strengthening the EAPs sanction and role
b. broadening access to employees
c. influencing policy makers
d. facilitating collaboration
e. developing strategic direction
f. promoting a proactive approach
g. integrating the EAP function

Risks are:

a. identification with adverse business decisions
b. diluting the EAP effort
c. confusing roles and boundaries
d. becoming involved with issues outside the EAP mission/mandate.

In South Africa, many EAP practitioners and occupational social workers are "stuck" in casework. To look at why this is so, it may be helpful to look more closely at the local research project referred to earlier. In this study, 70 occupational social workers were interviewed in 1989 and 1990. One question analyzed on what direct service the social workers spent the majority of their time. Results were as follows: 78.6% of respondents spent the majority of their time on casework; 7.1% on education and housing; 4.3% respectively on administrative services, community work and group work while 1.4% spent the majority of their time on research. There are many reasons for this emphasis on casework. At a practical level social workers often have enormous pools of employees to serve; for some as many as nine thousand. Thus, large numbers of employees seek individual help which creates large caseloads, with little time to plan and execute a change of focus. Also, the expectation of the majority of managers is that the service represents counseling/casework. Importantly, it was frequently how employees defined the source as well: individual, confidential counseling. Practitioners in sensitive areas such as the police force often made the point that employees would refuse to work together with colleagues on a common problem in order to protect their anonymity. Indeed, some respondents defended their focus on casework arguing that casework services individuals' particular needs; anonymity is guaranteed; if practiced well, casework can have an educational component and teach people life and problem solving skills–in other words, counseling can take on a preventive focus; further it can address the psychological problems frequently presented by employees; in large organizations counseling offers the employee the opportunity to be individualized and heard; and finally, casework/counseling can represent a vehicle for identifying and addressing collective issues.

Where respondents were unhappy with their casework/counseling response to problems they cited the following reasons:

- casework tends to deal with symptoms and not causes;
- at the workplace short term casework is the norm and thus deeper issues cannot be addressed;
- late referrals result in crisis intervention with no time to offer life skills;
- casework cannot deal with broader, macro issues;
- in certain organizational cultures, casework can make the employee feel exposed, singled out, and vulnerable.

Generally respondents wished to move toward macro practice with its potential for prevention. However, six respondents noted that management stresses the need for preventive work but they, the social workers, are stuck in the reality of casework/counseling; being on the shop floor, as such, they pick up the tremendous need for casework and are therefore committed to "employee oriented" direct services.

Two other themes of the research are related to macro practice: attitudes towards organizational change and attitudes towards becoming involved in work-related problems. With regard to the first, respondents were asked whether, in principle, organizational social workers should become involved in organizational change: 92.8% gave a firm commitment, acknowledging the role organizational stressors play in employees' problems. However, respondents did note some limitations in becoming involved in organizational change. These included:

- lack of social workers' knowledge, influence and experience;
- the fact that not all problems are caused by organizational factors;
- social workers are not always invited to play such a role and thus, opportunities for involvement are not provided;
- the principle of individualization: that is, setting changes for all employees may not be appropriate especially where the organization is spread out and needs differ.

Only 44.3% of respondents were actually involved in organizational change. When analyzing why this was so, two major trends emerged:

- the social workers' low status was a constraint; it removed them from decision makers and thus limited their potential for involvement in macro change;
- management had not sanctioned their role as organizational change agent.

With regard to work-related problems, respondents were asked in which work-related issues they became involved. Respondents saw opportunities for their involvement in such issues in the following circumstances:

- any work-related problem that included relationship and communication problems;
- any work-related problem in which individuals need to adjust to the workplace;
- where employees see social workers as more powerful than themselves there is a need for advocacy on behalf of the employees.

However, the following were reasons given for social workers not being able to become involved in work-related problems:

- social workers are seen as dealing only with individual issues and work-related problems are collective issues;
- social workers' core competency is therapeutic work; if other problems are tackled, boundaries with other professionals become blurred;
- the correct degree of integration into the organization may be lacking; this may be seen in the location of the social workers: for example, hostel-based social workers in the mines find it difficult to become involved in workplace issues.

- involvement in work-related problems may force the social worker to chose sides and respondents were wary of this;
- social workers are reluctant to tread on managers' toes and cause conflict because of the outcome (such as victimization) this could have on the employee.

In South Africa, with all the larger systemic problems we cannot afford to practice only with individuals. Too often, as social workers, we ignore the sociopolitical context of our work and certainly do not address the political implications of our practice. Often too caught up in the minutiae of practice, we fail to look beyond individual services. The official definition of social work in South Africa is "any act . . . treating social malfunctioning or problematic functioning in *man* or at promoting social stability in *man*." As one commentator pointed out, the legally directed focus for South African social work is adjusting the individual to the environment. The "person-in-environment" perspective appears elusive. As mature occupational social work and EAP practitioners, we cannot afford such a limited perspective.

REFERENCES

du Plessis (1991). The research here refers to the PhD study presently being conducted by the writer on Occupational Social Work in South Africa.

Ford, J.D. et al. "Organizational Wellness: New Slant for EAPs." *EAP Digest*, Vol. 6, No. 1, Nov-Dec. 1985, pp. 49-54.

Frank, R. and Streeter, C. "Identifying Roles for Social Workers in Industrial Settings: A Multi-Level Conceptual Framework." *Social Work Papers*, Vol. 19, 1985, pp. 14-22 and Bargal D. "Occupational Social Work: Report Based on Participants." Papers and Group Discussions: Proceedings from the International Expert Meeting on Occupational Social Work. Wassenaar, Netherlands, November 1987, *Eurosocial Reports*, No. 31, pp. 5-20, 1988.

Googins, B. et al. "Industrial Social Work in Europe," *Employee Assistance Quarterly*, Vol. 1, No. 3, Spring 1986, pp. 1-33.

Googins, B. "Occupational Social Work: A Developmental Perspective." *Employee Assistance Quarterly*, Vol. 2, No. 3, Spring 1987, pp. 37-53.

Googins, B. and Davidson (1989). "The Organization as Client: Broadening the Concept of EAPs." Unpublished.

Kurzman, P. and Akabas, S.H. "Industrial Social Work as an Arena for Practice." *Social Work*, Vol. 26, No. 1, 1981, pp. 52-60.

Ozawa, M.N. "Development of Social Services in Industry: Why and How" *Social Work*, Vol. 25, No. 6, 1980, pp. 464-470.

Santa-Barbara, J. and Coshan, M. "When the Workplace is the Cause of Stress" *EAP Digest*, Vol. 8, No. 3, March-April 1988, pp. 39-41.

Steiner, J.R. and Borst, E.C. "Industrial Settings: Underdeveloped Opportunities for Social Work Practice" *Arete*, Vol. 6, 1980, pp. 1-11.

Winkelpleck, J.M. "Directions EAPs Move: Evolvement Towards Organizational Methods." *EAP Digest*, July-August 1986, pp. 18-21.

Cultural Issues in South African EAPs: The Perspective of the Black Client

Mpholo S. Moema

SUMMARY. Cultural identity is at the core of the current socio-political changes taking place in South Africa. Similarly, EAP practice is fraught with obstacles that are culturally based, involve language barriers, traditional versus contemporary medicine, and even the use of marijuana for medicinal purposes. This article examines some of the cultural concerns facing black and white EAP practitioners and clients alike.

This article identifies and analyzes some of the cultural factors which commonly affect EAP practice in South Africa. These factors include the cultural conception of the EAP; the traditional belief systems; norms and values; the culture of migrancy and the legacy of a culture of apartheid.

As with all other secondary settings, occupational social work requires the blending of knowledge, values and skills. As Bopape (1988: 13) puts it, the actual blending of the three is initially artistic, and as such, no literature can prescribe the precise chemistry.

In comparison to other settings, occupational social work appears to tax the EAP practitioner's value base the most because the latter often relies heavily on the use of self as a tool for change. Du Plessis (1989: 3) correctly argues that in industry social workers, as contrasted with doctors, do not have access to medications to promote intervention and behavioral change. They depend, instead, largely upon the ability to build up trust and credibility among employees, and the organizational 'gamekeepers' who lend sanction to their practice.

Mpholo S. Moema is Senior Social Worker for the West Rand Region Gold and Uranium Division of the Anglo American Corporation of South Africa. He holds an honors degree in Social Work from the University of the Witwatersrand.

Experience gained so far on the South African occupational social work scene, particularly in EAPs, tends to show that it is mainly the recognition of the cultural component of the value base which determines the successful use of self as an agent of intervention.

CULTURAL CONCEPTION OF THE EAP

Black employees perceive the use of EAP within the context of their cultural system. As with any other group in South Africa, they are not averse to the idea of seeking help, nor to receiving help for personal problems experienced at the workplace. It is, in fact, in their nature to reach out for a resource outside self whenever they fail to cope.

However, it is important to note that when they use the EAP it is as an alternative to the network of traditional support systems that they employ in the first place. This perception is supported in a study conducted among Black mine employees by social workers attempting to set up an EAP in 1987. It was found in this study that, when confronted by social problems, the employees do not necessarily delude themselves into thinking that they can use escapist methods such as drinking, denial, sleeping, drugging, etc., neither do they keep the problems to themselves. Instead they deploy, as a first choice, a myriad of culturally significant figures of authority around them, such as relatives, home based peers, senior acquaintances, workmates, roommates, etc. It is only when these significant others are not available that they resort to the EAP as a resource (Moema et al., 1987).

It is therefore critical for the EAP practitioner to recognize the influence of these outside figures throughout treatment, because they continue to be used as a frame of reference. Motswenyane (1988: 5) argues that employees actually feel more at home with the treatment method that accommodates their belief systems.

THE INFLUENCE OF TRADITIONAL BELIEF SYSTEMS ON THE UTILIZATION OF THE EAP

Depending on their nature and location in South Africa, work organizations draw their workforce either from urban localities, or remote tribal homelands. This, in turn, determines the extent to which their EAPs are utilized by their employees. Unlike the retailing, commercial or manufacturing industry, which always deals with a more stable and homogeneous workforce, the labor intensive industries (such as the mines) often utilize sectors of labor which still adhere to traditional culture and primitive practices.

Traditional workers tend to believe that daily activities are influenced by one's ancestors. When he encounters a problem he believes that either his ancestors have cast a curse upon him, or someone is bewitching him. Conversely, when he is successful, it is not him but a supernatural power that is responsible. For this reason, it would not matter how successful the EAP program might be, and how much benefit the traditional employee might reap from treatment–he would still attach as much value to his indigenous forms of treatment. Such treatment normally occurs concurrently with, or after, EAP consultations, and is often carried out surreptitiously at night, in the neighborhood or back at home. Sometimes it is done purely as a complement to conventional EAP treatment. Tiba (1990: 19) argues that, because the health belief model of such employees accommodates strong cultural beliefs, recognition of these beliefs becomes important to the social worker when contact is made with the employee, since it may affect the employee's attitude and adherence to any prescribed treatment.

To illustrate this point, a brief case study is presented by Makeketlane (in Motswenyane, 1988: 6) of a patient who refused to take medication at a local mine hospital because he believed that the diagnosis made by the doctor was in no way related to his illness.

The employee was diagnosed as having gastric ulcers, a condition confirmed by his X-ray charts. During a discussion with the patient, it became clear that he did not agree with the doctor's diagnosis. He informed the social worker that he had once suffered from the same illness some years before, and had been treated by his traditional healer in his home town. Unfortunately, the treatment could not be completed because he had to return to the mines to renew his work contract. He believed he was suffering from what is referred to in the Sotho language as 'Sejeso.'

Sejeso could be any object, sometimes a living object, believed to have been implanted in a person's body by means of witchcraft. It is sometimes said to be physically felt by the affected person as it moves all over the body with the intention to kill.

The patient threatened to abscond or refuse hospital treatment in his belief that white medicine would never detect his real problem. After discussion with the doctor, it was agreed to allow him to go home for three weeks to attend to his problem. On his return to work he reported that he had been cured. He was then referred to the hospital for medical examination, and no trace of gastric ulcers could be found.

THE INFLUENCE OF NORMS AND VALUES

Sex and Age Taboos

In most South African Black cultures sex is taboo, and not considered a topic for open discussion. In fact, sex education traditionally was a function of the initiation school, a cultural institution outside the family. This poses problems when discussing sex related issues with a troubled employee. Where the practitioner is of a much younger age, and of the opposite sex, further barriers are created for EAP treatment around which the therapist has to find a way. Because wisdom is associated with increasing age, adults may disapprove of being addressed by a young person. Similarly, males may dislike being addressed by a female who is usually considered a perpetual minor. Thus, for one to earn credibility before such a group, Zazayokwe (1990: 8) says it is advisable to wear a uniform, a trademark of profession or authority, to help overcome discrimination against age or sex.

The Medicinal Use of Dagga (Cannabis)

In some of the remote rural areas of Natal, the Transkei and the Ciskei, dagga is grown and used like ordinary tobacco. Traditional healers from these parts of the country prescribe it medicinally (through boiling it in water and drinking the extract) to relieve asthma and the common cold. To employees steeped in this traditional practice, strong feelings against the EAP are bound to be stirred in the event of them being referred for dependency problems, because they often attach a conflicting value to the substance.

To illustrate the dangers of conflict of values, a brief case study, compiled by Mabe (1991: 8), is outlined below. It concerns a young Zulu hostel employee referred to a treatment clinic for a dagga dependency problem.

The employee's drugging history revealed that whenever he was ill he would be taken to a traditional healer, who, among others, prescribed dagga as a tonic. He started smoking dagga at the age of eight, and saw no harm in using it because, apart from the fact that it was grown in this area, his own grandfather and his father always smoked it as tobacco.

Upon admission, the employee did not understand that he had a dependency problem, and resented the idea of having to take (western) medication from the clinic's doctor because he had never consulted such a doctor before, and his parents also had not believed in such a form of treatment.

He flatly refused to stop using dagga, and this created a lot of tension between himself and the therapist.

The medical team's efforts to convince him that the use of dagga, either way, was harmful, and that it amounted to a violation of the treatment process, left the client withdrawn and closed during sessions. Although he attended sessions regularly, counseling and therapy had to be intensified to break through his cultural barrier.

The conclusion that is to be drawn from this case is that local cultural practices play a very important role among Blacks, and it would thus be detrimental to ignore them–even at the workplace. Respect for, and understanding of, the employee's social mores, norms and values is crucial to the realization of EAP treatment goals.

The Effect of a Culture of Migrancy

Until recently, as a result of the country's national social policy, more than half a million Blacks were employed as migrants in the South African mines. Hundreds of thousands more were in industry and commerce. Despite recent changes in labor laws, it is inevitable that for the foreseeable future and perhaps even permanently–migrants will continue to make up a substantial part of the workforce of South Africa.

Over the years this migratory labor system has led to the development of a single sex culture in hostels housing male employees to which EAPs have had to adapt. However, the family, as a unit, among Black employees, as with any racial group, plays a vital role in EAP rehabilitation. When dealing with the alcoholic, for example, research indicates that the best confronters, apart from employers, are spouses and other family members (Johnson, in Dichman et al., 1985: 107).

The absence of their families within the locality of the workplace has meant that troubled employees, during and after completion of EAP treatment, are returned unsupported into the same defective socio-cultural milieu that precipitated their breakdown. Unless the program enlists the aftercare support of culturally significant others, such as home-based peers, roommates, workmates, etc., the treated employees face high probabilities of relapse. Whether or not such EAP programs have organizational or systemic change on their agendas, the fact is by improvising, through the use of a somewhat less than ideal support system, the programs have effectively applied Band-Aids to cracking walls.

This apparent "collusion" with the system has not left the EAP practitioners, particularly the Blacks, unscathed. It is the continuous necessity to make up for the family when dealing with the "employee-as-a-person" that has, over the years, presented the social workers with the dilemma to bridge the yawning gulf between "moral" employee relationships and the "immoral" national social policy. Their consciousness was raised by the fact that the employees themselves have been defying the system by transplanting their spouses from the homelands, and settling them illegally around the workplace.

Language as a Cultural Barrier

All Black EAP practitioners are multilingual. Even before they begin schooling, Black practitioners usually speak two or more languages since they are influenced by several factors, such as difference in ethnicity of mother and father, neighbors (serving as playmates), tradesmen who have dealings with local people, church, and at times, government authorities. At school each is further subjected to two (official) additional languages, and these are seldom well mastered and they merely add to the multilingualism of the practitioner (Malaka, 1990: 4).

A conspicuous problem of multilingualism is noted among EAP practitioners who conduct interviews in the various languages of the employees they serve, but have to record in English. Some elementary words, in particular those denoting various shades of feelings (for example–depression, frustration, disappointment, etc.) do not exist in any Black language. The same goes for technological concepts such as virus, immunity, condom, T-cells, etc.

Such lack of concepts does impinge on effective EAP practice because the practitioner's ability to effectively use some interviewing skills is impeded. For example, when reaching for or wanting to stay with a feeling, the interviewer is often called upon to describe, or use phrases equivalent to, instead of using one word to denote the feeling. Malaka (1990: 15) has found that during social work training, students often exaggerated, when recording feelings, because of a lack of appropriate concepts. Feelings such as disappointment or depression are often all recorded simply as "uncooperative," etc., whereas these are often well explained when done in the language of the student. Obviously, pressures at the workplace do not afford the practitioner such luxury, but one is left to ponder the frustrations that are often generated by this gap in language communication between the user and the provider in EAP practice.

In the area of counseling, technical concepts such as virus, condom, immunity, T-cells, etc., do not exist either. To prevent possible miscommunication, Zazayokwe (1990: 8) suggests the use of relevant analogies and visual aids. With reference to AIDS, for instance, the immune system would be compared to an army which defends the body against invaders like HIV. Several terms could be used to denote a condom. Terms such as "raincoat," "rubber," "hard hat," etc., for condoms are often easily understood. Even for terms like "EAP therapist" or "social worker" analogies have to be contrived–for example to denote a social worker in the mining industry the term "Hlalakahle" (roughly translated as a neutral helper) is used.

Illiteracy

A poor educational background often results in a variety of practical problems. Low levels of sophistication among Black employees, as opposed to their white counterparts, often makes it difficult for them to conceptualize a therapeutic group, for example, as a valuable medium through which they could achieve change. They usually find it too abstract to comprehend until a lot of leading is done for the group by the therapist.

In AIDS counseling, Zazayokwe (id: 8) has found that some females do not encourage their partner to use condoms, simply because they lack adequate knowledge about the human anatomy. They maintain that death may result from a condom that has accidentally slipped off. An example is referred to in a training session of a female who feared she could be suffocated if the condom strayed to her lungs or some major life-supporting blood vessel. In such an instance, a visual aid illustrating the reproductive system of a female does help to alleviate ignorant reactions to using a condom for safer sex.

THE EFFECTS OF A CULTURE OF APARTHEID

Lack of Welfare Resources

There is no doubt that South Africa is presently steering away from its outdated apartheid economic system, and this change is beginning to be felt even in the workplace. However, for EAPs, this change leaves behind a legacy of a welfare system that is not only poor, but, in the words of du Plessis, is based on a specious philosophical premise absolutely naive to a developing country like South Africa (1989: 3). Inadvertently industry, and therefore EAPs, particularly those based on an off-site model, inherit a welfare system that is not only often inaccessible to it, but can seldom address work-related problems. Welfare resources are sparse and, where available, they discriminate against Black employees.

The result is some EAPs that are described as successful in South Africa–for example, the Anglo American West Rand Region Program–devote a large proportion of their intervention to macro issues. In this manner the EAP programs get their companies, through their corporate social responsibility programs, to improve, or even help cultivate, new community resources.

Supervisory Resistance

In the EAP field itself, it is inevitable that, despite the legal phasing out of the abhorrent apartheid economic system, attitudes and perceptions from both sides of the employee populations will for a considerable length of time continue to be jaundiced.

Because white supervisors traditionally have shown less liberal attitudes to Black employees than management, the latter's recognition of the need for EAP services to stabilize the Black labor force continues to be undermined down the line.

Lipton (1980: 134) observes, with regard to the mining industry, that among the obstacles to ameliorating the treatment of Black employees, have been the attitudes and behavior of white supervisors. Mining companies determined to bring about improvements have appointed new men to key positions and conducted re-education programs among the others. Many of the white employees who attended the courses describe them as "brainwashing sessions."

Concomitant with long held prejudices and negative attitudes, white supervisors will threaten, or even recommend for dismissal, Black poor job performers, rather than refer them to the EAP program for possible help. One of the reasons why some of the EAPs still suffer from this kind of supervisory resistance is because Black employee organizations are not yet partners to the programs.

Racial Barriers in Counseling

As indicated previously, apartheid, as a political ideology, has been a structure of laws, designed to guarantee white supremacy. Out of this doctrine a festering master-servant culture was thus legally perpetuated.

In EAP counseling the above culture of rigidly segregated worlds between Black and white employees is still the order of the day. Known for its conservative tradition, the mining industry is one major culprit in this regard. The Chamber of Mines still provides a counseling program within racial boundaries. What is more, because most EAPs in the mines serve exclusive racial groups, EAP Action Committees responsible for their maintenance are formulated and administered along racial lines.

All the above social engineering seems to engender feelings of insecurity, inferiority, subservience, non-assertiveness and possible self hatred in Black EAP practitioners. Mathabe (1988: 26) argues that, against this background, it seems feasible to expect obstacles, at least initially, in the establishment of a therapeutic relationship between a Black South African psychotherapist and a white client. How the obstacles are worked through, she asserts, will differ with individuals.

To illustrate these racial barriers in counseling, a group of South Africans were asked to write about significant accounts of contact with white clients in the United States. The following are written testimonies of two of these case studies presented by Mathabe (31-35):

> In group counseling practicum sessions I was always conscious of my Blackness. Whenever someone tried to reflect my feelings I would become tense, uncomfortable and defensive. As might be expected, I experienced a lot of uneasiness when I had to reflect others' feelings. It always scared me to see my clients blush. Fortunately, or unfortunately, the same reaction could not be seen in me. Nevertheless I did experience the same.
>
> It was not easy for me to establish a warm relationship with my clients because whatever the client did was not considered a normal reaction. For some reason, I perceived my client's reactions in a subjective manner. This formed a stumbling block in the relationship.
>
> Maintaining eye-contact was also a problem at the beginning. My experience had taught me never to "eye-ball" a white person. Having had bitter experiences as a result of looking Whites in the eye, I had difficulty using this technique. However, I have adjusted and can cope with almost any counseling technique.
>
> This adjustment was not without pain though. Most, if not all, of the problems I experienced can be attributed to the conditions under which I was compelled to live prior to my coming to the United States.

In another case study, a social work student writes:

> As a student I had to attend board meetings. Mr. "X" was assigned to take me to those meetings. He did that only once. All other times he would forget, and never apologize. He did not even tell me about his forgetting. I was instead told by a senior staff

member. The situation made me angry: I concluded that this was done out of arrogance, and the fact that I was a South African Black, and, hence, incompetent!

CONCLUSION

With urbanization the convergence of different ethnic and racial groups at the workplace has resulted in a love-hate diffusion of their cultures. Given that cultural influences and their accompanying traditional remedies cannot be discounted, the road ahead for the EAP field is riddled with challenges to identify those cultural issues relevant to dealing with mental illness.

In carrying out its function to stabilize the Black workforce in the new South Africa, EAPs have to come to terms with the values in their culture.

As R. Huws Jones aptly puts it "A man's values are like his kidneys, he hardly knows he has any until they are upset" (in Bopape, 1988: 13).

REFERENCES

Bopape, M. (1988). *South African Black Social Workers' Association*, Vol. 5, Lovedale Press.

Dickman, J.F., Emener, W.G., & Hutchinson, W.S. (1985). *The Troubled Person in Industry*. Illinois: Thomas Publishers.

du Plessis, A. (1989). *Report on Social Work Within the Gold Division of Anglo American Corporation of SA* (unpublished).

du Plessis, A. (1990). *The Relevance of Social Work in the Mining Industry* (unpublished).

Lipton, M. (1980). *Optima*, 29(3), 1980.

Mabe, M. (1991). *The Centre*, 8(2), Johannesburg: SANCA.

Malaka, D.W. (1990). *South African Black Social Workers Association*, 6(2), Westro Press, 1990.

Mathabe, N.R. (1988). *Racial Barriers in Counselling–The Case of a Black South African*. Braamfontein: Skotaville Publishers.

Moema, M.S. et al. (1987). *Survey into Attitudes of Black Mine Employees Towards EAPS* (unpublished).

Motswenyane, B.P. et al. (1988). *Social Work Practice*, 1, 1988.

Tiba, MA.E. (1990). *Social Work Practice*, 2, 1990.

Zazayokwe (1990). *Social Work Practice*, 2, 1990.

Ethical Issues in the South African Workplace

Shirley Thompson

SUMMARY. Ethics and values are at the core of social work practice. The article examines the ethical conflicts inherent in working in an environment sanctioned by apartheid. The author identifies the many areas of conflict and discusses how EAP practitioners must "position" themselves for ethical practice and avoid cooptation by the organization.

To understand the ethical dilemmas of service providers in the workplace it is necessary to give a brief history of social work in the workplace and the socio-political setting in which this has taken place. During the 1950's and early 1960's a process of social engineering entrenched and legalized what is commonly known as "apartheid." Separate residential areas, migratory labor, job reservation, especially in the mining industry, as well as a poor educational system not compulsory for the Black majority led, not only to a total lack of awareness of the problems and needs of the vast majority, but also to monumental social problems which are only now being tackled.

Prior to the early 1980's, social workers, occupational health nurses and other professionals were to be found in the larger institutions and industries. Their task was mainly to act as welfare officers seeing to the basic needs of employees such as accommodation, medical care or handouts from the welfare fund. Some crisis intervention counseling took place but with a lack of community resources, ongoing professional help was

Shirley Thompson, BA(SS), is EAP Consultant with The Centre for Occupational Social Work, a division of Family Life Centre, Johannesburg. This private welfare agency provides EAP and other services in companies in the Johannesburg area on a contracted basis.

available only to the privileged few. Some industrial alcohol programs were successful but did not gain a strong foothold in the business sector.

The mid 80's saw the emergence of trade unions as a credible force. Workers were made aware of their rights to equal pay and equal opportunity forcing management to see their workforce as people with needs and aspirations similar to their own. It was during this time that employee assistance programs (EAPs) became established as an additional benefit for employees. Moving into an area where paternalism was a norm the struggle for an identity separate from that of management was, and still is, a major task of the EAP and occupational social workers.

SOUTH AFRICA TODAY

In 1991 the last bastions of apartheid, namely the Group Areas Act and the Population Register Act, were repealed. Before the full effects can be experienced many structures will have to be dismantled. Given this, it can be envisaged that occupational social workers will still be limited in their function in many settings. State, para-statal health and mental health institutions are either totally or partially dependent upon state funding. Consequently, the system of separate services for different population groups is firmly in place. The employee's right to see an EAP counselor of his choice may or may not be possible depending upon how the services are organized. In the mining industry there are thousands of workers, mainly migrants, who neither speak nor understand English or Afrikaans which remain the two official languages at present. Many more Black social workers will need to be trained to provide services in the employee's native tongue. This will not serve to perpetuate apartheid but rather attempt to meet the challenges of reality. On the other hand, what of the educated Black mine employee? Will attitudes in this industry where values and beliefs are often at variance with those of the general community change soon enough for social workers to "not discriminate because of race, color, religion, age, sex, or national ancestry?"

South Africa is in the process of change and it is well documented in sociological studies that rapid change brings about instability. This instability is being manifested through fear, anger and violence. Expectations which cannot be met in the immediate future, an increased awareness of what the future may or may not bring have led to a sense of urgency for all those involved. A depressed economy is resulting in the closure of many small businesses, some large ones and ongoing retrenchments by those claiming to be struggling to survive. An additional factor affecting both employees and occupational social workers is the transferring of responsibility for welfare of individuals from the State to the private business sector.

Social workers in the workplace thus find themselves in a cybernetic system where the old patterns of organization attempt to maintain stability through the process of change and are faced with the dilemma of being perceived as disloyal to their employers when not aligning themselves with the forces maintaining stability, and as untrustworthy by employees and employee representatives when not aligning themselves with the process of change. The myth of a neutral stance or objectivity becomes even more of a myth when faced with the myriad of forces impinging on the worker. Keeney (1983: 77) in discussing self-reference says 'second-order cybernetics' places the observer in that which is observed. This will be discussed further when looking at changing situations in South Africa. For the moment the focus is on the current situation. To understand the dilemma of objectivity it is important to look more closely at the legacy of separate development.

Geographic communities in urban areas have developed in response to the availability of employment within a system of enforced association through ethnic origins. These communities comprise two to three generational urbanized families with many Western ideals and aspirations as well as newly arrived families from the rural areas who are still bound by their own culture and traditions. Under normal circumstances it is unlikely that such close association would prevail as each would choose neighbors and communities where there is more in common than the color of their skin. Added to these communities are hostels for single migrant workers whose families are many hundreds or even thousands of miles away. These workers are in, but not part of, the community where they live. Each member of the community fights desperately to maintain their own identity yet once in the office or more often on the factory floor they are seen as the 'workers' with little recognition of their differences and individuality. Supervisors might take the trouble to be familiar with their names, but it is not uncommon for them to be called John or Mary, whatever their name might be.

Family life has also disintegrated during this period of repression. Migrant workers living in the hostels see their families once a year during their annual vacation. The results of this enforced separation of the breadwinner from his family has had horrendous consequences. Alcoholism, promiscuity, both homosexual and heterosexual, gambling, and now AIDS are prevalent. It is little wonder that the hostels are seen as breeding grounds for violence.

For those more fortunate there is a semblance of family life although it often falls far short of what Western society considers healthy and normal. Both parents leave home long before their children go to school; small children are left with their older siblings to care for them, or left with an aged care-giver. When the parents arrive home late at night there is little time for family interaction and families become disorganized with older children seeking alternative structures in which to develop. These may be friendship groups, street gangs or political groups.

One must also consider the effects of enforced separation on the privileged sector of the community. The so-called white South Africans have also been denied the opportunity to mix freely with their fellow South Africans. Admittedly, this enforced separation made life less complicated and helped to maintain feelings of superiority and power, but today the white man knows far less about his black compatriot than the black man knows about him and his culture. As the managerial class, with only a few exceptions, is made up of white personnel it is little wonder that much fear and confusion exists when considering all the implications that change will bring about.

Finally, there is a desperate shortage of community resources with both the government and private sector having to concentrate on housing and education to make up the mammoth backlog. Health services and private welfare agencies are severely affected by this situation and services are either being contracted or in some cases suspended. The consequence of this situation is that the occupational social worker is often so overwhelmed by the volume of work at a micro level that it becomes almost impossible to deal with macro issues.

Candace Bibby in her article, "Reviewing the Counseling Component" states "Now more than ever, the employee assistance program (EAP) practitioner is being called on to review the utilization of treatment resources, to negotiate preferred provider arrangements, and/or to provide gatekeeping responsibilities." It is regrettable that the South African practitioner is unable to attain this goal in the prevailing situation.

It is with this background that one must consider the functions of EAPs and the role of the occupational social worker.

CURRENT ETHICAL ISSUES

The basic value of social work and the cornerstone of the profession is the dignity of the individual and his or her right to self-determination. The academic training of every social worker in this country is built upon this value. The NASW Code of Ethics has been the foundation of all our ideals. Ethics are meaningless, however, when experienced as a concept. Meaning can only be assigned to ethics when expressed in action. As opportunities arose for social workers to enter the workplace many saw this as their chance to work in consonance with their beliefs and values. In addition, it was an opportunity to work at bringing about change without fear of falling foul of the authorities with possible detention for "subversive activities." Few envisaged the many obstacles to be overcome.

ROLES AND FUNCTIONS

Roles and functions may differ from one setting to another depending upon a variety of factors. These include:

1. How the initial decision was arrived at to employ a social worker or to implement an EAP. It may have been a management decision:
   - to provide a service to assist employees who are seen to be troubled;
   - as the result of a field placement by one of the academic institutions which was experienced as beneficial to that company;
   - resulting from approaches made by individual social workers to human resource departments in an attempt to market their services;
   - following the recommendation of one influential person on the management team who is attempting to change attitudes regarding the basic rights of employees.
2. Unions employ social workers for the benefit of their members.
3. Management's perception of the problems in the workplace. This is closely linked to whether they are willing or able to view employees from an ecosystemic viewpoint. More frequently the troubled employee is seen as someone whose problems stem from intrapsychic causes.

Ethical issues can arise when the occupational social worker sees her own ethical base being challenged by management. One example of this is where a social worker was bargaining for some relaxation on office employees' starting time due to large distances to be traveled, need to get children to schools and nurseries and long lines for transportation. Employee representation was minimal in the company concerned and previous approaches by employees to their immediate supervisors had been unsuccessful. If an employee was late on more than three occasions, disciplinary action was instituted in strict accordance with the Labor Relations Act. The procedure is to give one verbal warning, two written warnings, followed by dismissal if the 'problem' of late-coming persists. The social worker argued that the employees had found a solution to the problem which would in no way affect the smooth running of the department; they were loyal, hard-working employees who had encountered this difficulty after moving into a middle-class area, further from the city, when home ownership became a reality. The majority had at least one car in the family, but as the company only provided parking for managers they were dependent upon public transportation. Management viewed the issue differently. They considered they had a responsibility to all employees to inculcate Western standards. They went even further by saying that they were helping employees to be prepared for running their own businesses in the new South Africa!

Although not an issue in the above example this may be the point to discuss work ethics. The Protestant work ethic brought into this country by European settlers and immigrants is firmly entrenched in the South African way of life. It is taught in the homes and schools and on entering the workplace the majority have incorporated this into their value system. To many of the indigenous peoples, it is a foreign concept and where young people enter the work market without any formal schooling, usually as unskilled labor, the meaning of work is to receive pay for the provision of shelter, food and clothing. As larger numbers have the opportunity to be educated, this gap will lessen, but it does serve to highlight the fact that values, and, therefore, ethics are constantly changing in response to changing attitudes, new situations and shifting priorities.

Confidentiality

Although management has accepted the concept of confidentiality as defined by social workers, problems are often experienced with middle management and supervisors. A long history of paternalism has made them experts over not only the working lives of their subordinates, but, also, their private affairs. The intrinsic power in this position makes it difficult for them to forego this role. As companies become less bureaucratic, they will acquire comparable power in areas linked to the policy and goals of the company. In the meantime, the social worker is often placed in a double bind as supervisors may refuse to refer an employee because they are not kept informed regarding the worker's difficulties.

Much education work has to be done to help them understand the individual's right to confidentiality.

Self-Determination

It is not unusual for managers and supervisors to become very skilled in "doing for," instead of helping the employee to work with and solve his problem. This easily leads to their taking over the responsibility of solving the issue. They may take over the finances and budgeting, visit an employee at home to help resolve marital difficulties or, if they feel the difficulty is beyond their capabilities, telephone the social worker to make an appointment on behalf of the employee. When it is suggested that the employee make contact they fail to see the reason even if an attempt is made to explain the therapeutic value of this requirement.

Non-Judgmental Attitude

South Africa lags behind the United States in its attitude towards alcohol problems. Despite educational and awareness programs, attitudes are hard to change.

Until recently, replacement of workers with alcohol problems was expedient. With the need for more advanced technical skills the alternative of treatment is being considered. In many instances, the decision to recommend treatment and assistance with reintegration into the workplace is taken by assessing the employee's value to the company rather than the needs of the individual. The behavior of the alcoholic prior to recognition of the problem provides ample reason for dismissal without mention of the real reason. Occupational social workers are seeing the introduction of alcohol policies as a priority in their work.

Individualizing

The degree to which individualizing is experienced is closely related to the context. In a sophisticated commercial setting with few workers who have not completed at least secondary education, individualization is of a high order. At the other end of the continuum is the mining industry which is not only one of the largest employers but also the industry with a majority of unskilled workers.

These workers originate from all parts of South Africa, have no common language and are called to shift by numbers. A simple language called Fanakalo has been devised to provide a medium for communication in the mines. Each group falls under the control of an Induna who has been appointed by their superiors. Due to ethnic and tribal differences the Induna may not be recognized as being in a superior position to them because of lower social standing in their own tribal community, or could be from a tribe which is seen as being inferior. The workers have no voice in these appointments.

Other issues which have caused occupational social workers to take a stand from their professional ethical base include being asked to act as replacement or 'scab' labor during industrial action, to intervene in labor disputes when strike action is threatened on housing issues, to encourage breathalyzer tests on entering the workplace, to report cases of homosexuality in security-sensitive settings, to name a few. The last two instances create dilemmas for both the social worker and for management, the one upholding values for the individual and the other concerned with the values of good management, responsibility to the whole workforce, and society in general.

THE OCCUPATIONAL SOCIAL WORKER IN A CHANGING SOCIETY

What has already been written could be construed as a rather negative picture. This is not necessarily the case. There are many challenges facing the occupational social worker who enters the workplace with a sound generic training, an ability to work at both micro and macro levels, an awareness of the many forces impinging on both the worker and the setting and a good knowledge of occupational social work as practices in both America and Europe. At the same time, this information has to be used in such a way as fits the present situation with its specific and often unique problems. du Plessis (1990) writes:

> one of the strengths of occupational social work is that it can be tailor-made to suit each employing organization. Social work within a large single sex hostel for migrant workers on a remote mine will therefore differ enormously from efforts within an urban capital-intensive computer company, or a trade union. Factors affecting practice include prevailing socio-political and economic conditions; the employing organization's "agenda" and values; expressed and felt needs of consumers and potential consumers as well as the social worker's own personality and training.

du Plessis later states,

> Another point to be made is that the group of occupational social workers is not an homogeneous one. Practitioners span all race groups, political persuasions and ages. Some are committed to "working for management," defining the employer as the focus of accountability. Others are attempting to gain legitimacy with different interest groups. Some practitioners are content to limit their role to personal counseling while others are trying to broaden their base.

Generally, it is acknowledged that the occupational social worker is accountable to her or his employer, to the employee as client or potential client, to her or himself and, finally, to the profession. Googins and Godfrey (1987) ask: "To whom does allegiance belong? The client? The employer? The profession? What are the limits of intervention? What treatment methods are available and effective? What responsibility do social workers have for advocacy and systems change?"

Before accepting an appointment the social worker needs to inform the potential employer of the ethics of his/her profession, how these may differ from those of other professionals within the organization and how these will affect the way in which she works, her accountability to others, as well as management, and spell out in detail his or her conception of confidentiality. Having done this the social worker can enter the workplace without what could be perceived as a "hidden agenda." Should the employer, which is in most instances management–as union initiated social work positions or EAPs are only just being considered–require the social worker to practice his/her profession at a micro level, undertaking mainly personal counseling? This need not be a deterrent. The good occupational social worker will soon gain credibility and be recognized as an integral part of the organization. The way will then be open to make suggestions and implement programs dealing with the real issues which often precipitate the manifestation of troubled employees.

Keeney (1983) says "the notion of objectivity with its accompanying regard for self-reference often prevails in man's dealings with human systems." Within this context we must acknowledge the value systems internalized by individual occupational social workers. The nature of change initiated in the workplace will be influenced by the occupational social worker's ethnic origins, social, economic and political experiences and beliefs as well as the manner in which these have been integrated into the basic ethics of social work practice.

Akabas and Kurzman (1982) in defining "What's so Special?" note that "Service through the workplace provides access to large numbers of persons and to organizations with influence. The resultant opportunities, which are multiple and multi-layered, can be a strain as well as strength."

We argue that for the practitioner, and for the profession in general, entry into these institutions may be best accomplished through the core social work practice function of direct service. This role allows the social worker to become invested in helping, establishes the professional as concerned with individuals, reduces the danger of promising more than can be delivered and delineates a turf that may not have been staked out earlier by other persons in the workplace. From this solid base of internal power, derived from professional expertise, the social worker then is able to build trust and make use of the profession's full repertoire of knowledge and skill–the key assets of which, in the world of work, are its understanding of person and environment in interaction, its commitment to individual growth, and to social change.'' This encourages the occupational social worker to look beyond the provider of direct services and gives encouragement to work towards change in society through the workplace.

REFERENCES

Akabas, S. H. and Kurzman, P. A., eds. (1982). *Work, Workers and Work Organizations: A View from Social Work.* Englewood Cliffs, N.J.: Prentice-Hall.

Bibby, C. (1990). Reviewing the Counselling Component. *EAP Digest*, September/October 1990.

Compton, B. R. and Galaway, B. (1975). *Social Work Processes.* Homewood, Illinois: The Dorsey Press.

du Plessis, A. J. (1990). *Social Work in Action*, ed., McKendrick, B. W. Pretoria: HAUM Tertiary.

Googins, B. and Godfrey, J. (1987). *Occupational Social Work.* Englewood Cliffs, N.J.: Prentice-Hall.

Keeney, B. P. (1983). *Aesthetics of Change.* New York: The Guilford Press.

Alcohol and Drug Abuse: Treatment Alternatives in South Africa

Lee Wilcocks
Laura Edmonds

SUMMARY. This article provides an overview of alcohol and drug problems in South Africa. The authors identify the social and economic implications of the most commonly abused drugs and penalties for offenders. Intervention methods enforced by the court system are also examined. Additionally, the current status of chemical dependency treatment and self-help groups is discussed.

South Africa is an extremely complex first and third world society with its population of some 26 million (1985 census) representing at least thirty different ethnic and cultural groups.

Historically the use of chemical substances, primarily alcohol and marijuana, has been an integral part of South African society since its earliest

---

Lee Wilcocks holds a Bachelor of Social Science Degree from The University of Capetown, an Honours Degree in Psychology (1982) and a Masters Degree in Industrial Psychology from Rand Afrikaans University (1986).

She has been involved in the field of alcohol and drug dependence for the past 24 years. She was previously Deputy Director for SANCA Job Services, responsible for the supervision, training and functioning of five clinics. In 1989 she was appointed Chief Executive of Riverfield Lodge.*

Laura Edmonds graduated from the University of the Witwatersrand with a degree in Social Work (1982). She commenced employment at SANCA Job Services and was promoted to the position of Superintendent in 1985 and Manager of Clinical Services in 1987. Since October 1989 she has held the position of Clinical Manager at Riverfield Lodge.

*Riverfield Lodge is a subsidiary of Lifecare Clinics, Ltd. It is the first multiracial chemical dependency treatment center to open in South Africa.

days. The problems associated with the use and abuse of chemical substances only began to receive official attention in the late 1960's and early 1970's, when legislation was promulgated to deal with "the drug problem" in South Africa.

Consequently, despite having a chemical substance problem of some magnitude, research into the extent of the problem and the development of preventive and treatment facilities is in its infancy.

LEGAL DRUG ABUSE

Alcohol Use and Abuse

Alcohol is available legally in all parts of the country through licensed outlets to any person aged 18 years or older. Figures compiled by the Human Sciences Research Council in 1986 indicated that approximately 75% of the adult population were users of alcohol and that approximately 700,000 alcohol users were either alcohol dependent or potentially alcohol dependent.

Groups who have been newly identified as having increasing rates of alcohol dependency through their referral to treatment centers in the recent past include:

- young (18-25 year old) Black people who, due to political turbulance and upheaval have received limited education and have poor employment prospects;
- adolescents of all population groups.

Due to limited public education and knowledge of alcoholism, only a fraction of the estimated alcohol dependent population have submitted themselves for treatment. It is suggested that the full extent of the problem will only become apparent once community education is provided on a large scale.

Prescription and Over-the-Counter Drug Abuse

The lack of central controls over the purchasing of "legal drugs" such as prescribed drugs and those available at all pharmacies, makes this area of chemical dependency very difficult to assess. While the Medical Control Council of South Africa schedules and sets limits on the sale of all psychoactive (as well as other) substances, there is no form of control at the outlet, meaning that people are able to obtain drug supplies with relative ease.

South Africa is a very chemically oriented society due to alternative lifestyle management skills not being established here as yet.

Numerous substances are readily and cheaply available for all ailments (whether physical or emotional) and widespread abuse, evident from the large proportion that this group of chemical abusers make of treatment center admissions, is common.

According to P.A.D.A. (Pharmacists Against Drug Abuse–an organization formed to address the problems of legal drug abuse), the most commonly abused drugs are benzodiazapines (Valium and Ativan), substances containing codeine, appetite suppressants and cough preparations.

ILLEGAL DRUG ABUSE

Marijuana "Dagga" Abuse

The production of "dagga" (the local term for cannabis or marijuana) has developed into a massive illegal industry in South Africa. Estimates are that the industry is worth some R12 billion annually (4.8 billion US equivalent)–about 10 times more than the large local sugar industry is worth.

In 1989, 4,000 tons of dagga were seized world-wide and of this haul 1,100 tons were from South Africa.

The climate in many parts of South Africa is ideal for the cultivation of dagga and this, combined with limited infrastructures and accessibility to many areas, has made controlling the industry a near impossible task.

Of importance is the fact that the dagga grown in South Africa has a T.H.C. (Tetrahydrocannibol) level some 10 times higher than that grown in Europe and the United States. Consequently, higher levels of intoxication are reached with its usage.

The use of dagga, which is available cheaply and easily, is widespread among all sections of the South African population. Many mystical and magical properties are assigned to it and its use is culturally acceptable to some groups.

It is the most favored "recreational" drug among high school pupils with 20-30% using it at least once during their high school careers. Combined with the widespread use and resulting complications of dagga abuse is the highly specific South African problem of dagga and mandrax (methaqualone) abuse. This practice became popular some 15 years ago and involves the combined smoking of dagga and crushed mandrax tablets–usually in broken-off bottle tops called white pipes. Methaqualone, despite having been declared a banned substance in the 1970's is easily available in the country and is either smuggled in or manufactured locally in sophisticated illegal laboratories.

The smoking of the "white pipe" enhances the effect of dagga and gives the user a brief "rush" before depressing the central nervous system. High levels of tolerance to this mixture develop and cases of addicts smoking 40-50 tablets daily are not uncommon.

Youth from all population groups are involved in this practice and it is estimated that approximately 50% of all admissions to drug treatment centers among the 15-25 year age group are due to this form of addiction.

The social problems associated with the "white pipe" usage are vast and include strong links to crimes such as housebreaking and prostitution.

Opiate Abuse

South Africa has, until recently (1985), remained relatively heroin free. However, addicts are now beginning to present themselves at treatment facilities and the amounts of heroin being confiscated are escalating–indicating that the international drug syndicates are beginning to infiltrate a fresh and eager market.

At present the most commonly abused opiate in South Africa is a synthetic substance known as Wellconal (a trade name for a substance containing dipipanone hydrochloride and cyclizine). Despite stringently enforced controls of the substance, which is used medically for the relief of severe pain, an enormous trade in the substance exists with prescription forgeries and pharmacy break-ins being the primary means of obtaining it.

The drug is administered intravenously under unsterile conditions, frequently with tragic consequences. Many Wellconal addicts have lost limbs due to developing deep vein thrombosis and gangrene. Frequent deaths have also occurred due to accidental over-dosage of the substance–in 1988, 30 deaths were recorded and numerous others suspected of being Wellconal related.

The effects of, and problems associated with, the drug have been linked to those of heroin and our experience has shown that treatment of the addiction is as difficult.

Volatile Solvents

Volatile solvents are cheap and easily available in South Africa and a large number of young people abuse them. Types of volatile solvents abused include glues containing toluene and acetone, aerosol sprays, eraser fluid, lighter fluid (butane), benzine, ether and gasoline.

Of serious concern is the widespread epidemic of glue sniffing among very young (5 years onwards) children from the lower socio-economic groups. Frequently these children are homeless and become street children addicted to cheap "shoe makers"-glue which they describe as taking away their hunger and providing them with an escape from their desperate circumstances. Groups of street children are a common sight in South Africa's main centers where they beg or steal to obtain the few cents required to buy them enough glue for their next high. Death due to asphyxiation or Sudden Sniffing Death (S.S.D.) occurs frequently, as do severe physical problems of organic brain damage, blindness and paralysis.

Cocaine Abuse

South Africa has, until recently, remained cocaine free, yet an epidemic of massive proportions is predicted as the market is a fresh one and is being saturated by international markets. Recently (April 1991) a R1.26 million (approximately $500,000) haul of pure cocaine was made. Cocaine remains expensive in South Africa (R200-R300 per gram) ($80–$120 US equivalent) and consequently the use is restricted to the upper socio-economic groups. Users are usually high functioning, wealthy and frequently professional people.

Treatment centers are noting an increase in the numbers of people admitted for cocaine abuse–this increase is predicted to rise sharply within the next 12 months as the full impact of the problem establishes itself.

While isolated incidents of crack abuse have been noted, this problem is not of note at present, but it is predicted that the lower socio-economic groups will provide a vast market once the cocaine market is established.

THE LEGISLATION

Legislation was promulgated in South Africa in 1971 to deal with various aspects of the problems of chemical substance abuse. This Act, known as "*The Abuse of Dependence Producing Substances and Rehabilitation*

Centers Act," Act Number 41 of 1971, is still, together with various amendments to it, operative.

Statutory Treatment Committal Procedures Without Criminal Involvement

The most significant feature of Act 41 of 1971 is that it makes provision for involuntary consent. This provision was devised on the premise that the chemically dependent person is frequently unwilling to submit him/herself for treatment or is unable to make a rational decision regarding receiving treatment.

This procedure as outlined in Act 41 of 1971 is called *committal* and the process, safeguards and controls ascribed to the procedure are outlined in the Act.

Prior to the holding of a *Committal Inquiry* various "evidence" has to be presented to a court of law. Such evidence includes the sworn declaration by any person who knows the chemically dependent person well to the effect that the person is chemically dependent and in consequence thereof squanders his means or injures his health or harms the welfare of his family, a psycho-social report by a registered social worker into the circumstances of the individual, and a medical report.

Once the court is satisfied with the evidence presented to it, the chemically dependent person is summoned to appear before the court for the inquiry to be held. Such inquiries are held "in-camera" and the subject of the inquiry may appoint legal representation, bring witnesses, cross examine witnesses and give evidence on his or her own behalf. Should the court be satisfied after the proceedings are complete that the person is chemically dependent and would benefit from treatment, the person is ordered to present him/herself for treatment at a designated rehabilitation center.

Admissions to treatment centers in terms of this procedure, are until such time that the person is considered to be ready for discharge by the management of the center. Should a period of longer than 12 months be required, additional permission has to be obtained from the legal authorities concerned. On discharge from the center, a process of "Release on License" is instituted. This means that various conditions are attached to the discharge–usually including ongoing supervision by social workers. Licenses can be revoked and the person returned to the center if conditions are broken. This procedure is non-criminal in orientation and no criminal record is attached to its implementation.

There are obviously numerous civil rights issues attached to this process. However, if used appropriately, it becomes an effective means of coercing a chemically dependent person to receive treatment *when all other methods have failed.*

Statutory Treatment Procedures with Criminal Involvement

The Criminal Procedures Act, Number 51 of 1977, makes provision for conversion of criminal proceedings into Rehabilitation Inquiries. This section (255) applies in criminal proceedings where the judicial officer presiding at the trial may, with the consent of the prosecution and in consultation with a social worker, stop a criminal trial where he believes the accused person to be chemically dependent and convert the criminal trial into a Rehabilitation Inquiry (as outlined above). All criminal trials, with the exception of those which carry a sentence of death, may be converted in such a manner.

Further provision is made in the Criminal Procedures Act (sections 296 and 297) for criminal sentences to be postponed or suspended conditional on whether or not they were drug dealing in South Africa. This alteration became necessary as many people given the mandatory 5 year sentence were, in effect, drug users rather than drug dealers.

Dealing, including the manufacture or growing of illegal drugs, is now subject to a fine of R30,000 ($12,000 US equivalent) or 15 years imprisonment or both and second or subsequent offenses to a R50,000 ($20,000 U.S. equivalent) fine or 25 years imprisonment or both.

Possession of Drugs

Possession of illegal drugs carries a R20,000 ($8,000 U.S. equivalent) fine or 10 years imprisonment or both for a first offense and R30,000 ($12,000 U.S. equivalent) fine or 15 years imprisonment or both for a second or subsequent offense. These sentences can be postponed or suspended conditional on the person receiving treatment for chemical dependency.

TREATMENT SERVICES IN SOUTH AFRICA

The treatment of alcohol and drug dependence in South Africa began in 1956 when, after a visit by Marty Mann from the U.S.A., the first information office was opened in Johannesburg. This was the birth of the South African National Council on Alcohol Dependence (S.A.N.C.A.)–later to become S.A.N.C.A.D. with the addition of drug dependence.

S.A.N.C.A. grew over the years and at present has 23 societies throughout South Africa. Each society is autonomous and provides differing services ranging from in-patient and out-patient treatment to information and education only. These societies are subsidized by the Department of Health Services and Welfare.

The Department of Health Services and Welfare has also established several treatment centers of their own, which tend to take patients who are "committed" under the Abuse of Dependence Producing Substances and Rehabilitation Centers Act 41 of 1971 and who are not expected to pay for their treatment. Several treatment centers are also funded by various religious organizations, who, if registered under the Act, also get assistance from the Department of Health Services and Welfare. Basically, anyone can set up a treatment center, but must be registered by the Department of Health Services and Welfare and meet their criteria. In 1989 the first private treatment clinic opened. Riverfield Lodge, a Subsidiary of Lifecare Clinics, Ltd., is the only private multi-racial treatment center specifically established for the treatment of alcohol and drug abuse dependence in South Africa.

Until recently there has been much duplication of services due to separate facilities for different race groups. However, over the past ten years out-patient services particularly have become multi-racial, although most in-patient clinics remain race specific. The new clinic is geared for the upper income group of all races who felt ill at ease in the "welfare" type clinic. There is a paucity of treatment centers in South Africa–particularly for the black population who need treatment programs specifically geared to their needs, cultural heritage and beliefs.

TREATMENT MODELS AND RESOURCES

The various treatment facilities in South Africa offer different services; even those such as S.A.N.C.A.D., although grouped under a national umbrella, are autonomous in their functioning. Most institutions grow out of the needs of their community, but owing to a lack of funding do not always function optimally.

In-Patient Treatment Programs

In-patient programs range from 5 day detoxification to 14, 17, 21 and 28 day treatment programs. State institutions, taking committed patients, have programs which range from 6 weeks to 6 months but are less therapeutically intensive. Adolescent in-patient drug programs are usually longer ranging from 6 weeks to 3 or sometimes 6 months. Most in-patient programs are followed by aftercare programs of varying intensity and structure.

Out-Patient Treatment Programs

Out-patient programs operate in the cities and are often attached to hospitals in the rural areas. In the cities, out-patient programs usually require daily attendance for the initial 3 months in order to monitor withdrawal medication during the first 2 weeks and the administration of Antabuse on a daily basis thereafter. Attendance then reduces to 3 times a week and continues to decrease until by 9 months the patient only attends once a week, but is encouraged to continue Antabuse on a daily basis for the first year. Individual therapy usually takes place on a weekly basis for the first 2 months and reduces depending on the patients' needs and progress. Group therapy and educational groups supplement the out-patient programs. During the second year the patient continues to attend the clinic as he sees fit, but maintains at least monthly contact with his therapist. After two years of sobriety the patient is discharged but may continue to keep contact if he/she wishes.

Aftercare

Aftercare or ongoing care following discharge from an in-patient treatment program varies from one clinic to another. For many it means attending out-patient groups at the clinic on a weekly or bi-weekly basis. At some clinics it entails attendance 3 times a week to take Antabuse plus one group a week. The most comprehensive aftercare program at present is that devised by the new private clinic which, because it caters for people throughout South Africa and neighboring states, has a network of private therapists in all areas to whom it may refer patients after discharge for ongoing therapy. In this case, therapy is recommended for a 2-3 month period on a weekly basis, decreasing according to the patient's progress. Attendance at by-weekly groups at the clinic is also part of the aftercare program as is attendance at A.A. and N.A. groups on a weekly or twice weekly basis.

Self-Help Groups

A.A. has increased considerably over the years in South Africa and has, at present, 234 groups and a following of an estimated 7,000 members. Although not as all-pervasive as the American A.A., they are the major self-help and support group for alcohol dependents. Many clinics include A.A. groups in their programs and encourage patients to continue attendance once discharged.

Families are encouraged to join Al Anon and there are a few Alateen groups in South Africa. In the major cities, finding an A.A. group to go to 3-4 times a week is not difficult. Rural areas present a problem and members may have to travel quite a distance to attend an A.A. meeting once a week.

N.A. groups have been struggling to establish themselves for the last 7 years and a handful have finally managed to get going–these are in the 4 major cities.

There is obviously a need for A.C.A. groups, but to date only one has been recently formed. Also burgeoning over the past 3 years is the Tough Love movement, which is helping many families with young drug dependents. Family support groups have sprung up in one or two cities. In general, however, self-help groups have not yet reached the proportions that those in the U.S.A. have attained.

ASPECTS OF ALCOHOL AND DRUG DEPENDENCE TREATMENT

In some respects the focus of treatment in South Africa differs from that of many overseas treatment facilities in that the main focus tends to be therapy orientated rather than exclusively addiction orientated. Patients in treatment institutions are counseled by professionals. This is mainly due to the fact that for many clinics, positions and not patients are subsidized and these positions must be filled by registered social workers or psychologists. As psychologists are more expensive than social workers the subsidized welfare organizations mainly employ social workers. Subsidies for these positions are usually not comparable to salaries in the private sector and therefore the organizations have to supplement the subsidy in order to remain competitive with other employers. Therefore, all welfare organizations have to raise monies in addition to their subsidies.

What this has meant in practice is that these organizations have not been able to employ recovering addicts as counselors, as they would not be subsidized. A further implication of not employing recovering addicts is that the treatment programs either do not include A.A. steps and traditions at all, or have varying degrees of A.A. theology included in the program. Most in-patient clinics have a visiting A.A. group which patients attend on a weekly basis and thereby get their introduction to A.A. and are encouraged to join their nearest A.A. group once they leave.

Treatment programs vary in duration, intensity and quality, making it difficult to give an accurate overview. However, the more professional in-patient clinics have programs that would include the following:

An assessment interview, training for families in intervention and confrontation techniques, a medically supervised detoxification period, education groups–focusing on addiction, and skills orientated groups which will help the dependent to cope with life situations in the future without chemicals. These would be stress management, assertiveness training, communication and relationship skills, psychodrama, self-management and dysfunctional families.

The treatment regime also includes: self awareness and self esteem groups aimed at improving the patient's concept of self worth, chemical dependency groups, often confrontational in nature, family education groups, family therapy groups, relapse prevention groups, individual therapy–which is normally fairly directive and uses behavioral techniques and rational emotive therapy, depending on the therapist's training, and individual family therapy sessions. Occupational therapists are highly trained in South Africa and are often responsible for conducting the stress management, assertiveness and psychodrama groups.

In addition, treatment programs often include relaxation techniques, sport and physical training, creative therapy, music therapy and art therapy which is the responsibility of the occupational therapist. Aftercare groups run by the clinic and aftercare referral to community resources are also integral components. Out-patient treatment programs do not have the intensity or the variety of groups and tend to concentrate on the detoxification followed by individual therapy on a weekly basis and a weekly group. Most out-patient clinics experience difficulty in getting patients to groups due to working hours, distances and lack of after hours transport facilities. Having had contact with and knowledge of treatment clinics and personnel in Britain, Europe and the United States, it would appear that treatment services in South Africa in general compare favorably with those overseas. There is strong emphasis placed on ongoing training of professional staff, which keeps them abreast of international developments and knowledge.

Unlike the United States, however, probably the biggest restraining factor on the development of staff and services has been, and remains, lack of state funding.

In the private sector, the development of highly professional but relatively expensive clinics is hampered by the fact that very few of the over 400 Medical Aid funds (government funded health care) will pay for the treatment of alcohol and drug dependence. Most have exclusion clauses or very low annual limits. Insurance medical plans also exclude alcohol and drug dependence. This means that in most cases the patient is totally responsible for the payment of the treatment.

ALCOHOL AND DRUGS IN INDUSTRY

The EAP movement gained momentum in South Africa in the late seventies. At that time, some of the American companies–such as Ford and A.E.C.I. had alcohol policies which they inherited from their parent company, but these were somewhat vaguely implemented. Much of the pioneering work had begun in the mining houses earlier on–a particular group had built their own alcohol/psychiatric treatment facility for their workers.

Initially, programs focused on alcohol, but rapidly broadened and became fully fledged EAPs with a broad brush approach.

The implementation of programs and treatment varied depending on the company and community resources.

The choices available to companies with alcohol and drug patients, identified through the EAP were as follows:

1. To send the patient to a community resource, either in-patient or out-patient.
2. To have an in-house model where the company is large enough to employ an occupational nurse, a doctor and a counselor/social worker.
3. To have an assisted in-house model where the company doctor and occupational nurse handle the medical aspects, i.e., medical examinations, monitoring of withdrawal, withdrawal medication and administering Antabuse daily, and the patient receives counseling from an outside source–either at their offices in the community or the counseling resource sends a social worker on a weekly basis to counsel all the patients on the program.

Wilcocks, who implemented some of the first successful EAPs in South Africa and who was employed by a community resource, found that the assisted in-house model was the most suitable. This enabled an outside resource, specializing in EAPs, to train supervisors and health personnel and educate the workforce and monitor the patient referrals and the program through the contracted social worker(s). The community resource was also able to provide social workers most suited to the cultural and language needs of the patients. Much of South Africa's labor force consists of unskilled black migrant laborers from the adjacent homelands and neighboring countries. Many do not speak English and maintain strong cultural identities that white South Africa has not incorporated into treatment because of the racial segregation promulgated by apartheid.

Many of the other programs lost their impetus because the treatment component was not satisfactory. Either the community resource was not satisfactory or the company's own counselor was not trained in alcohol and drug counseling.

The assisted in-house model allowed the community resource to keep a finger on the pulse of the EAP and to monitor the patients in treatment. This model also ensured that the patient didn't get lost between being confronted and referred to the treatment resource. Liaison between supervisors and social workers was easier and the co-ordinating team, i.e., the doctor, nurse and social worker and an elected member from management, were all able to meet regularly and provide mutual support.

CONCLUSION

The EAP field in South Africa still has a long way to go. One of the future developments will be the contracting of companies with treatment centers to treat their employees. Clinics with the EAP expertise will become involved in the company's EAP in terms of consultation, training and education, as well as being responsible for the actual treatment of alcohol and drug dependence.

This area is likely to be the main stimulus for growth in the treatment services for alcohol and drug dependency in South Africa in the next decade. Being accountable to commerce and industry for services rendered promises to improve the professionalism and efficacy of the treatment services.

Minimizing Post Traumatic Stress in Critical Mining Incidents

J.C.C. Badenhorst
S.J. Van Schalkwyk

SUMMARY. Mining is the predominant industry in South Africa. It is also one of the most dangerous. This article discusses the development of a post-traumatic stress and accident involvement program developed by the Chamber of Mines of South Africa as a result of an explosion in a mine shaft that cost the lives of 52 employees.

Research findings have resulted in society's increased awareness of the pressing need not only to address the physical effects of a traumatic event, but also the psychological effect that it has on victims. COPE (Care of Pressurized Employees) describes how critical incidents in the South African mining industry can be managed more effectively as an Employee Assistance Program endeavor toward increased organizational efficiency and effectiveness in human resource management.

TRAUMATIC INCIDENTS IN THE MINING INDUSTRY

Annually large sums of money are invested in the implementation of safety systems within mines, audits to test effectiveness, first-aid training, publications on mine safety, and the administration of mine safety competitions (Chamber of Mines of South Africa Publication, 1989) in an at-

---

J.C.C. Badenhorst is Director of COPE, the critical incident program developed for the South African Mining Industry by the Chamber of Mines.

S.J. Van Schalkwyk is Senior Management Consultant with SANLAM Insurance Company and has been involved in critical mining incident management in the South African mining industry.

tempt to circumvent the detrimental occurrence of critical incidents in the South African mining industry. The aforementioned activities are directed at the establishment and maintenance of a safety system that would be conducive to the prevention of accidents within the mining environment. The Fatality and Reportable Injury Rates with regard to employee loss during critical incidents in the South African Mining Industry (Chamber of Mines Report, 1991) is prominently displayed in Table 1.

TABLE 1

FATALITIES, REPORTABLE INJURIES, FATALITY RATES AND REPORTABLE INJURY RATES OF THE MEMBER MINES OF THE CHAMBER OF MINES OF SOUTH AFRICA

Year	Fatals	Reportable Injuries	Fatality Rate	Reportable Injury Rate
Gold Mines				
1984	592	13,528	1.27	29.01
1985	528	12,866	1.13	27.49
1986	681	11,321	1.45	24.09
1987	529	9,633	1.16	21.12
1988	496	9,430	1.08	20.45
1989	517	8,921	1.16	20.05
1990	522	8,055	1.24	19.17
Coal Mines				
1984	56	657	0.71	8.32
1985	32	523	0.46	7.60
1986	24	492	0.36	7.35
1987	96	397	1.58	6.53
1988	31	280	0.56	502
1989	26	269	0.46	4.76
1990	24	281	0.44	5.17
Total Mines				
1984	672	14,781	1.12	24.54
1985	586	14,118	0.98	23.56
1986	732	12,486	1.22	20.74
1987	665	10,648	1.14	18.19
1988	563	10,296	0.95	17.40
1989	589	9,800	1.01	16.07
1990	602	9,057	1.07	16.13

(Chamber of Mines, 1991)

It is disturbing to realize that 1 out of every 1000 employees were fatally injured in the mining industry during 1990 and that 16 out of every 1000 employees sustained injury that had to be formally reported to the Inspector of Mines. While these figures are relatively low when compared with international standards, the incidence of critical mining incidents remains a major cause of concern within the South African Gold Mining Industry. The effective management of critical mining incidents has therefore emerged as a key objective in the application of this industry's EAP technology.

The present mine safety approach compensates for the physical aspects of traumatic incidents only. Since psychological consequences of mining incidents remain undetected, many victims continue to seek medical treatment for physical complaints that lack an organic cause (Friedman, Framer, and Shearer, 1988). Research reveals that the vast majority of adults and children (victims, observers, and rescue workers) who were exposed to traumatic incidents, exhibited PTSD symptoms (Wilkinson, 1983; Tern, 1981). These findings are devastating when the detrimental effects associated with quality of life and work performance are fully comprehended. Individual reactions to the impact of traumatic incidents differ. Limited individuals exhibit no ill effects, some show immediate reactions while others respond with symptoms much later (6-12 months following trauma). Some individuals are affected for brief periods, while others are affected for long periods (10-15 years). Normally the magnitude of the physical impact is less important than those factors that affect the individuals' perception of the events and efforts to cope with the critical accident that occurred. More often, less significant incidents like near-miss situations, or being indirectly involved as observers, relatives, friends, colleagues or rescue workers stimulates PTSD, as defined in Table 2 (American Psychological Association, 1987).

PTSD IN THE WORK SITUATION

An extensive survey by the EAP Services Department of the Chamber of Mines (1988) indicated that PTSD often accounts for production variables that cause organizational ineffectiveness delineated in Table 3.

Cost Implications of PTSD

Friedman, Framer, and Shearer (1988) state: "Nothing threatens the achievement of a productivity mission and the resultant profits of an employer like an unhealthy workforce."

TABLE 2

SYMPTOMATOLOGY -- POST TRAUMATIC STRESS DISORDER

A. The person has experienced an event that is outside the range of usual human experience and that would be markedly distressing to almost anyone, e.g., serious threat to one's life or physical integrity; serious threat or harm to one's children, spouse or other relatives and friends; sudden destruction of one's home or community; or seeing a person who has recently been, or is being, seriously injured or killed as the result of an accident or physical violence.

B. The traumatic event is persistently re-experiened in at least one of the following ways:
- recurrent and intrusive distressing recollections of the event
- recurrent distressing dreams of the event
- sudden acting or feeling as if the traumatic event were recurring (includes a sense of reliving the experience, illusions, hallucinations, and dissociative episodes)
- intensive psychological distress at exposure to events that symbolize or resemble an aspect of the traumatic event, including anniversaries of the trauma.

C. Persistent avoidance of stimuli associated with the trauma or numbing of general responsiveness (not present before the trauma), as indicated by at least three of the following:
- efforts to avoid thoughts or feelings associated with the trauma
- efforts to avoid activities or situations that arouse recollections of the trauma
- inability to recall an important aspect of the trauma (psychogenic amnesia)
- markedly diminished interest in significant activities (in young children, loss of recently acquired developmetnal skills such as toilet training or language skills)
- feeling of detachment or estrangement from others
- restricted range of affect, e.g., unable to have loving feelings
- sense of a foreshortened future, e.g., does not expect to have a career, marriage or children, or a long life.

D. Persistent symptoms of increased arousal (not present before the trauma), as indicated by at least two of the following:
- difficulty falling and staying asleep
- irritability or outbursts of anger
- difficulty concentrating
- hypervigilence
- exaggerated startle response
- physiologic reactivity upon exposure to events that symbolize or resemble an aspect of the traumatic event.

E. Duration of the disturbance (symptoms in B, C and D) of at least one month.

Delayed onset if the onset of symptoms was at least six months after the trauma.

(American Psychological Association, 1987)

TABLE 3

PROBLEMS IN THE WORK SITUATION

1. ABSENCE FROM WORK
   - Excessive sick leave
   - Monday, after pay-day absenteeism
   - Absenteeism due to minor conditions
   - Unauthorized leave
   - Strange and unsatisfactory reasons for absenteeism

2. ABSENCE WHILE AT WORK
   - Continual absence from work place
   - Late arrival and early departure from work
   - Sleeping on duty

3. ACCIDENT RECORD
   - Accident proneness while on duty
   - Accident proneness outside the work place
   - Involvement of other employees in accidents
   - Near miss incidents

4. GENERAL INDICATORS OF DECREASED EFFICIENCY
   - Decreased concentration
   - Erratic work pattern
   - Decreased memory for instuctions and detail
   - Increased difficulties with complicated instructions
   - Inability to meet deadlines
   - High frequency of mistakes
   - Poor judgment and decision-making
   - Peer group complaints about work performance
   - Above average wastage of time or material
   - Unacceptable excuses for poor work performance

5. POOR INTERPERSONAL RELATIONS WITH EMPLOYEES
   - Over-reaction to real or imagined criticism
   - Sudden mood changes
   - Unwarranted grievances
   - Detachment from fellow employees
   - Increased hostility with fellow employees
   - Behavior that illicits unfavorable reaction

6. UNPRODUCTIVE BEHAVIOR/LEGAL MATTERS
   - Dangerous behavior (self and others)
   - Excessive alcohol usage
   - Increased involvement in legal matters

(Chamber of Mines, 1988)

If PTSD is not addressed appropriately, medical costs as well as staff turnover rates may increase drastically. The effect of early treatment on the costs associated with PTSD, has been well documented in the management of 200 clinical cases at the Barrington Psychiatric Center, Los Angeles, California (Friedman, Framer, and Shearer, 1988). Two hundred employees who had experienced a critical incident during working hours were divided into two equal groups (100 cases who were interviewed and exposed to professional intervention following the critical incident and 100 cases who received professional intervention 6-36 months after the critical incident). The latter group received treatment later since their symptoms were initially undetected. The costs associated with PTSD (disability, litigation, treatment, rehabilitation, and lost time at work) were averaged for both groups.

Findings clearly indicated that early detection of PTSD and prompt referral intervention resulted in significant savings. While the average total cost associated with the early detection of PTSD cases was $8,300, the average total cost for PTSD cases with delayed detection and intervention amounted to $46,000. PTSD cases who experienced delayed identification and intervention incurred more than five times the rehabilitation costs of those who received intervention shortly following the critical incident.

Employees who received prompt intervention demonstrated an average 12 week recovery period and a low incidence of permanent disability. Employees who received delayed intervention required an average 36 week recovery period and presented with negative effects in the long-term. Only 13 employees of the group who received prompt intervention chose to litigate, whereas 94 of those who experienced delayed intervention sought redress. The tendency toward litigation is manifest in the fact that victims of trauma often desire revenge. If the normal focus for revenge is absent, the employing organization becomes a natural target.

Decreased litigation following trauma among employees who received prompt intervention may be associated with employees' apparently feeling that their employers cared for them, enhancing their sense of loyalty and decreasing their need to litigate.

The preceding findings clearly show that early identification of PTSD and prompt referral for professional intervention, offers significant employer savings (decreased disability, litigation, less lost working time, as well as a reduction in treatment and rehabilitation costs). Many employees remain to suffer from the psychological effects of traumatic incidents long after the physical damage has been repaired. Since PTSD has a delayed onset in most instances EAP intervention aimed at preventing the unnecessary development of this condition among mining employees involved in critical incidents within the industry is crucial. In a production oriented climate such as the South African mining industry, a PTSD management system for the recapturing and preserving of the industry's manpower potential, serves the ultimate objective of productivity.

COPE: A FRAMEWORK

COPE was developed after a tragic mining accident at the St. Helena Gold Mine on the 30th August 1987 when 52 employees died after a methane gas explosion sent their cage to shaft bottom (DeBeer, 1988).

The name COPE, an acronym for "Care of Pressurized Employees," destigmatizes concepts like illness; disease and disorder were substituted with a positive message. The objective of COPE is to provide a management system which can:

- Assist employees in coping effectively with demands and pressures that adversely affect quality of life and production health during and following traumatic mining incidents.
- Provide employees who experience difficulties in coping with the effects of trauma, early access to professional care.

To encourage employees and their dependents to utilize COPE optimally, the program is supported by Mine Management in a Policy Statement (Table 4).

TABLE 4

COPE POLICY STATEMENT

The Management of this mine supports the COPE programme to assist employees and their families to manage with psycho-social problems which have adverse effects on their job satisfaction, quality of work, productivity and lifestyle. The following principles pertain:

1. Personal information of the employees utilizing the program will be kept strictly confidential;
2. Employees treated will receive the same consideration as those extended to employees with medical problems;
3. Participation in the program will not prejudice an employee's job security or chances of promotion;
4. Participation in the program is voluntary;
5. Management reserves the right to recommend employees for assistance;
6. The program should not be abused by employees.

COPE PROGRAM

The COPE Program operates in three modes:

Mode I: Care of Employees Pressurized by a Past Critical Incident

Since many employees have been killed or injured in critical mining accidents in the past, PTSD is commonly found among the members of a mine work force. The COPE Program therefore includes a component for the identification, referral and treatment of such individuals.

The industry EAP service of the Chamber of Mines which renders a daycare psycho-social service at its Regional Centers for Human Development in the major mining regions in South Africa are best suited for the treatment of Mode I cases. These Centers have at their disposal the services of psychologists, social workers, and psychiatrists in multi-disciplinary and multi-cultural fashion.

The mine in-house EAP infrastructure, which operates on many mines is the most practical solution for the management of employees in need of Mode I assistance.

The in-house EAP infrastructure of individual mines, an extension of the existing mine managerial function accepts responsibility for:

- The establishment and maintenance of a system by which employees suffering from psycho-social problems can be identified and referred for appropriate assistance; and
- The implementation of a PTSD preventative program at mine level in consultation with Regionalized Centers for Human Development.

The Mode I operationalization of COPE requires that all mine employees be oriented in COPE and EAP. The level of training input employees receive is determined by their specific role with regard to COPE. While all employees need a basic awareness of these programs, employees on supervisory level receive training in identifying pressurized employees and referring such persons for treatment to Regional Centers for Human Development or other appropriate community resources. Since supervisors' role in the identification of PTSD-affected employees is based on production criteria, they need not be trained as lay diagnosticians.

Mode II: Care of Employees Involved in Minor Critical Incidents

A minor critical incident is not defined in terms of the intensity of its effects on an organization, but in terms of the degree to which it disrupts employees within the organization in which it occurs. In the event of a minor incident the ordinary support systems of both the organization and employees are still intact and fully functional. Since many individuals involved in minor incidents show no immediate stress reaction (delayed nature of PTSD) the Mode I infrastructure's reactive characteristics are not sufficient to deal with employees needing assistance. In such instances the COPE Program should also intervene on a proactive level. For this reason specific mine employees (preferably from the manpower departments) are nominated as "COPE Agents" and trained in the basic identification and referral of affected employees.

Following all minor incidents "COPE Agents" should actively identify, interview and refer employees who were involved in, or exposed to the traumatic effects of critical mining incidents. The COPE Agent is responsible for decreasing resistance to proactive intervention before referral for tertiary assistance at a Center for Human Development or a relevant resource in the mining community.

Mode III: Care of Employees Involved in Major Critical Incidents

Major critical incidents disrupt the functioning of an entire mine to such an extent that the whole operation and existing support systems are adversely affected. Since major critical incidents in mines are unpredictable (impact of destruction–people, material and existing infrastructure) Mode III management of PTSD requires that mine management follow specific procedures in order to cope effectively with the critical incident and its sequelae.

During a major critical incident an attempt should be made to interview all involved (victims, colleagues, observers, rescue workers and families) and refer specific cases for professional intervention, as in Mode II. During a major critical incident the functions of the COPE Agents (Mode II) and the Supervisors (Mode I) remain similar ensuring a system conducive to the continuous identification, referral and treatment of employees who may develop PTSD at any stage.

During major critical incidents affected individuals can be managed in groups on site by staff from the Regional Center for Human Development. Center for Human Development staff can be consulted by mine management on human behavior issues concerning the macro management of the critical incident. Since trauma related circumstances can make intervention impractical, the collective addressing of all involved through alternative mediums after the critical incident provides an opportunity to address the following issues:

- An atmosphere of motivation and coping with the critical incident is facilitated.
- Mine management's acknowledgement of the human response to critical incidents is demonstrated.
- Rational perception of the events can be stimulated among all parties involved.
- Employees and their families can be reminded of how to deal with and where to receive personal assistance regarding PTSD.

The effective systems management of employees following exposure to a critical mining incident is dependent on important trauma management principles. They are:

1. Simplicity:

Any intervention strategy aimed at assisting employees following a critical incident should be as simple as possible. The following guidelines pertain:

- physical comfort, consolation and protection from further harm.
- reunification with natural support systems.
- encouragement in the ventilation of feelings and experiences.
- stimulation of rational perspective (providing the real facts).
- education regarding human reactions to trauma.
- stimulation of realistic and constructive activity.
- encouragement of coping behavior.
- focusing on inner strengths and potential.
- continuous stimulation of hope.

2. Proximity:

Support should be provided as close as possible to the disaster scene by utilizing individuals from normal support systems such as family, friends, co-employees or supervisors to render the necessary bio-psychosocial assistance.

3. Immediacy:

Trauma management should be rendered as soon as possible after the critical incident has occurred.

4. Expectancy:

Resumption of normal duties and activities as soon as possible following the traumatic incident is the major objective of management. The expectation should be that recovery is possible through the utilization of personal coping skills and potential. A sick role (patient status) should never be ascribed to any employee who has been exposed to a traumatic incident (Kleu, 1979).

CONCLUSION

Every employee in an organization is prone to involvement in a critical incident. Trauma, no matter what the nature of intensity, has detrimental consequences for both the employee and the organization. Trauma affects each employee and all the systems which he forms a part of, in a multitude of ways. Physical, emotional, social and vocational aspects of life and living are disturbed or disintegrated. Trauma creates an economical and emotional burden for the employee and organization since it impacts directly on organization productivity.

Since a traumatic incident within a mine has such extreme consequences on the individual, group and system levels it is fitting that attention be given to its effective prevention and management by means of holistic interdisciplinary planning and intervention. The EAP service rendered by Regionalized Centers for Human Development to mines in the South African Mining Industry provides the best solution providing those employees who have been traumatized in critical mining incidents, with an opportunity to get back into the mainstream of positive production health with the least negative consequences.

The mining industry's long-term commitment to employee well-being and the industry's continuous acknowledgement of the value that Employee Assistance and Regional Centers for Human Development has for the preservation of quality human resources is exhibited in the utilization of COPE during critical mining incidents.

REFERENCES

American Psychiatric Association. (1987). *Diagnostic and statistical manual of mental disorders*, 3rd ed. Washington, D.C.: APA.

Chamber of Mines of South Africa. (1989). *Mine safety division, mining survey*, 3, 8-9.

Davison, G.C. & Neale, J.M. (1986). *Abnormal psychology: An experimental clinical approach*, 4th ed. New York: Wiley.

DeBeer, D.W. (1988). Enkele kommunikasie perspektiewe na aonleiding van die Kinross en Sint Helena Mynrampe. *IPM Journal.*

EAP Service Department of the Chamber of Mines of South Africa. (1988). *Employee assistance programme: The role of the in-house EAP co-ordinator and EAP action committee*. Johannesburg: CM.

Friedman, R.J., Framer, M.B., & Shearer, D.R. (1988). Early response to posttraumatic stress. *EAP Digest*, September/October, 45-49.

Kleu, A.H.P. (1979). *Opernsionale wanfunksionering: 'n psigodiagnostiese–dinamiese studie*. Unpublished MA Thesis, University of Pretoria, South Africa.

Mine Safety Division of the Chamber of Mines of South Africa Report. (1991). *Death and injury rate tables: Gold, coal and other mineral mines*. Johannesburg: CM.

Wilkinson, C.B. (1983). Aftermath of disaster: The collapse of the Hyatt Regency Skywalk. *American Journal of Psychiatry*, September, 140, 1134-1139.

Enuresis Among Black Mining Employees: A Preliminary Study

J.C.C. Badenhorst

SUMMARY. Enuresis is a problem often associated with childhood. In the South African mining industry it is a prevalent concern of miners living in employer-owned hostels (work site dormitories). This article discusses a study of this phenomenon and seeks to establish its causation. The author also addresses the potential role of employee assistance programs in helping employees and employers in dealing with this problem.

Enuresis among Black adult male employees living in mine hostels is a phenomenon of concern for the individual, fellow residents, hostel management and EAP therapists. This article discusses the findings of a preliminary study on a sample of 21 employees with bedwetting problems. Demographic, work related, health and psychosocial information is provided. Suggestions are made with regard to the management of this condition in the mining environment as well as further research on this phenomenon.

Enuresis, the repeated inappropriate involuntary passage of urine, is a well known and albeit embarrassing condition which has been documented as far back as 1500 B.C. Enuresis is most popularly believed to be bio-psycho-social in nature with definite indications that developmental factors (effective bladder control in 3rd year of life) rather than psychodynamic factors are causative. Generally associated with childhood, more prevalent

J.C.C. Badenhorst is Director of COPE, the critical incident program developed for the South African Mining Industry by the Chamber of Mines.

in boys than in girls and more often nocturnal in nature the occurrence of enuresis in adulthood is not uncommon.

Friedman et al. (1975) indicate that the persistence of enuresis into adolescence is related to:

- passive-aggressive, passive-dependent reactions
- past history of sleepwalking
- family history of sleepwalking
- inferior dentition as measured by decayed, filled or missing chronic genitourinary tract complaints (urgency, frequency nocturia)
- family history of enuresis.

The development of enuresis in adolescence after a period of dryness (secondary enuresis) is most often caused by transient emotional stress such as the adjustment to military service, home sickness, fatigue, examination anxiety or emotional turmoil. Findings that have been made with regard to nocturnal enuresis are that it is less likely to have any associated or causative organic pathological basis, its prevalence is characterized by a disproportional large number of delinquents. Psychosocial associations with regard to bedwetting are that it is more common in winter and in cold than heated sleeping quarters and also characteristic of heavy sleepers. Despite difficulty in proving clinically that psychological disturbances are related to enuresis, psychological interventions are meaningful in some instances.

Findings indicated that an unaccepting attitude to the occurrence of enuresis is detrimental to the cessation of the habit. Reassurance, support and anticipation of relapse episodes are fundamental elements for treatment success. Effective management of enuresis varies from placebos, conditioning devices, psychotherapy, pharmacology, bladder training and sleep interruption to hypnosis.

ENURESIS AS AN EMPLOYEE PROBLEM

Within the gold mining hostel residence system the incidence of black male employees with persistent bedwetting behavior has given rise to concern. Besides difficulty in the effective management of the condition the occurrence of bedwetting within the hostel system is an unhygienic, embarrassing and interpersonally menacing phenomenon for the individual, roommates and hostel management.

Since various potential physical, social, cultural and lifestyle stressors interplay within the specific working and living environment of black mining employees the need for the verification of this phenomenon is evident. Against the background of limited information on the specific phenomenon and the relative incidence of enuresis in the adult population it was decided to conduct a pilot study as a first step in the establishment of an adequate data base for subsequent research.

PILOT STUDY

The bedwetting population (21 subjects) of a specific mine hostel was utilized for the implementation of the study after a formal request for EAP intervention by mine management. There were initially 21 participants. At the end of the study, 1 subject died, 1 subject objected to participation, 2 subjects went on leave, 4 subjects absconded from the physical examination, and 13 subjects completed the entire study.

The bio-psycho-social nature of enuresis resulted in the implementation of a systematic and structured evaluation process to determine the existence of potential causative factors that may be conducive to the condition within the hostel residence as subsystem of the mining environment.

Consultation, consent and collaboration between personnel management, the medical superintendent, hostel medical station personnel, hostel management and Centre for Human Development staff resulted in the gathering of the various indices of information as a basis for profile establishment of the sample population.

- Demographic information: age, ethnic group, marital status, educational level.
- Work related information: job category, work area, mine service, performance appraisal including conduct, complaint and disciplinary procedures were established from employee records.
- Health related information: number and reason for consultations, work related injuries, hospitalizations, the start of enuresis, severity of enuresis, possible reasons for enuresis, previous treatment, and medication were extracted from medical records.
- Physical condition information: each participant was medically examined and neurologically screened by a medical officer–at the Mine Hospital. Laboratory tests were conducted for the following:
  - Full Blood Count
  - Microscopic Cell Count
  - U + E and Creatinine
  - Gamma Glutomol transpeptidase (GGTP)
  - Cannabinoids

- Psychosocial information–a questionnaire was completed for each participant, providing details on feelings, thoughts, fears, selfconcept, interpersonal relationships, behavior and psychosocial symptom items.

All information was systematized and integrated. The data was interpreted qualitatively and where possible quantitively (Table 1).

ANALYSIS OF RESULTS

The population studied was a representative sample of the hostel residents. Since the size of the sample population creates a bias with regard to the incidence of enuresis among the different ethnic groupings generalizations in this respect should be avoided.

Work related information is indicative of increased conduct and complaint incidents among the sample subjects despite the reporting of satisfactory work relationships and job satisfaction in the majority of cases. This finding resembles research on nocturnal enuresis being present in a disproportionate large number of delinquents (Friedman et al., 1975). The high incidence of AWOP's and subjection to disciplinary procedure of varying intensity also supports this finding. The specific influence of alcohol abuse in the causation of numerous conduct complaints must also be considered.

Quantitative analysis indicates that a large number of the sample population have a relative short mine service record suggesting that the incidence of enuresis may be ascribed to the process of adjustment to the mining environment. Job stress, more specifically the psychological perception of loss risk (injury and death) which is linked to deeplevel (1-4 miles) gold mining must be taken into consideration. The effect of fatigue in a physical working environment where the primary emphasis is on production may be a factor of concern.

Health related findings indicate that in this group enuresis is a problem with an average duration of 26 months. This finding correlates with the relatively short mine service of sample subjects studied. Physical examination indicates that the sample subjects have causative organic pathology. Commensurate with literature, genito-urinal tract infection was present in the majority of the sample subjects. The high incidence of genito-urinary tract problems may be ascribed to the high incidence of alcohol abuse as substantiated by the sample subjects self rating of the primary reason for their bedwetting, alcohol related complaints (3/21), increased S-GGTP scores (7/13), incidence of sexually transmitted disease (5/21), and the mean duration of enuresis (26 months).

Alcohol abuse may be related to emotional turmoil that is experienced in the mining milieu with its associated physical, psychological and social stressors. The evidence of these stressors is aptly represented in the psychosocial findings. Information on specific symptomatology, feelings, thoughts, fears and images as reported by the subjects in the sample population pertain. Separation from traditional support systems and the effect of transcultural transition could be considered as causative of transient emotional stress.

While generalizations with regard to the underlying reasons for bedwetting within this specific population may be difficult various assumptions seem evident. Despite the indication that organic pathology is absent in some of the cases the exclusion of this as a cause by thorough medical examination as soon as possible after primary detection is essential. Among the subjects in the pilot study the role of alcohol abuse as a major contributory factor in the occurrence of bedwetting is the most prominent and most closely associated with the magnitude of conduct and complaint incidents that have been encountered among sample subjects. The consumption of large quantities of traditional beer and the simultaneous effect of alcohol on sleeping pattern and moral value systems is evident.

While a combination of psychosocial stressors may be contributory of alcohol abuse it is evident in this study that the effective management of alcohol abuse is essential in the secondary prevention of bedwetting. Effective prevention of alcohol abuse or successful alcohol abuse rehabilitation of subjects with bedwetting may have significant effect on the prevalence of bedwetting among employees within the hostel resident system. Since positive feedback between the relation of alcohol consumption and bedwetting has been reported in the present alcohol rehabilitation program this matter may have to be further researched. The possible effect of increased transient emotional stress among bedwetting subjects needs consideration too. The stress levels of bedwetting subjects may be affected by the risk to health and threat of death in deep level mining on the one hand and the specific stress of living in an isolated community away from family support systems for long periods of time on the other hand.

CONCLUSIONS

While the author is aware that factors such as the size of the sample and the qualitative nature of the pilot study may be insufficient to permit the formulation of objective conclusions the specific findings of the study

TABLE 1

Findings

Demographic	Sample Population	Hostel Population
Mean Age:	33.6 years	35 years
Age range:	26–50 years	20–60 years
Marital status:		
- Married	76%	70%
Ethnic Grouping:		
- Basuto (3,7/1000)	19% (4)33.5% (1081)	
- Xhosa (7.8/1000)	38% (8)31.5% (1915)	
- Tswana (9.2/1000)	24% (5)16.7% (538)	
- Shangaan (9.7/1000)	9.5% (2)6.4% (205)	
- Swazi (13.6/1000)	9.5% (2)4.6% (147)	
- Pondo	0	3.2% (104)
- Zulu	0	2.5% (81)
- Pedi	0	1.4% (46)
- Other	0	0.2% (5)
- TOTAL	100% (21)	100% (3222)

Work Related

Work area:		
- Underground	85.7	89.4
Average Mine Service:	3.9 years	12 years
Conduct or Complaint incidents:	17/21	-
- AWOPS	13/21	-
Subjection to Disciplinary procedures:	16/21	-
- Warning	9/21	-
- Severe Warning	3/21	-
- Final Warning	4/21	-

Work Relationships: All Subjects indicated satisfactory work relationships.

Job Satisfaction: Two of the thirteen subjects indicated that they were dissatisfied with their job.

Health Related

Duration of Enuresis:	
- Range	2 - 128 months
- Average	26 months

TABLE 1 (continued)

Health Related	
Magnitude of sick reports:	
- Range	1 - 52 occasions in total period on mine
- Mean	20.5 occasions in total period on mine
Self rating on alcohol abuse as the primary reason for enuresis:	13/13
Alcohol related complaints:	8/21
Alcohol related assaults:	6/21
Sexually Transmitted Diseases:	5/21
Physical Condition	
Neurological Screening:	1/13
U + E and Creatinine:	12/13
S GGTP:	7/13
Cannabinoids:	2/13
M C S:	9/13

Psychosocial Profile

- Symptomatology: the majority of subjects rated the following symptoms as being experienced frequently -

headaches	appetite problems
sleeplessness	backaches
early morning waking	

- Feelings: the feelings most often experienced by subjects were indicated as being -

regretful	lonely
hopeless	depressed
helpless	unhappy

- Fears: the fears most often described by subjects all pertained to loss. The most prevalent fears in order of rank were -

death	loss of job
underground accident	loss of wife/girlfriend

- Thoughts: subjects most often indicated to having thoughts of being -

negative	unattractive
unlovable	worthless
inadequate	deviant
useless	life as being empty

TABLE 1 (continued)

Psychosocial Profile

- Images: subjects indicated that the images mostly experienced were -

pleasant sexual images	helplessness images
pleasant childhood images	loneliness images

- Self Image: subjects accounted self images of -

failure	hurting others
not coping	being followed
loss of control	being talked about
being hurt	being laughed at

- Family relationships: all subjects indicated satisfactory family relationships.

- Substances Abuse: the use of pain killers was indicated as being often while the use of alcohol was indicated as being regularly by all subjects.

do illuminate the phenomenon of bedwetting among black male mining employees.

In the absence of formal research information and culture free verification evidence the above presentation of basic information on bedwetting may be valuable for hypothesis formulation in multi-disciplinary research on the specific factors that interplay in the causation of enuresis within this specific population of employees in the South African gold mining environment.

In an attempt to manage enuresis more effectively with the hostel system an EAP for bedwetting residents is proposed (see Chart 1). It is envisaged that this proposal be accepted by Mine Management and implemented in hostels as a standard operational procedure.

CHART 1. PROPOSAL: EAP for Bedwetting Residents in Mine Hostels

PHASE 1	PHASE 2		PHASE 3	
DETECTION	ASSESSMENT	OUTCOME	MANAGEMENT	RESPONSIBILITY
	Comprehensive medical examination	Pathology	Physical treatment	MEDICAL STATION MINE HOSPITAL
		No pathology		
	Assessment of alcohol consumption	Abuse	Alcohol rehabilitation	HOSTEL MANAGEMENT HOSTEL SOCIAL WORKER
		Non abuse		
	Evaluation of psychosocio-cultural status	Stressors	Stress management	HOSTEL MANAGEMENT HOSTEL SOCIAL WORKER HEALTH EDUCATOR

REFERENCES

Backwin, H. & R.M. Backwin: *Behaviour Disorders in Children*, W.B. Saunders Company, London. 1972.

Friedman, A.M., H.I. Kaplan & JB J. Sadock: *Comprehensive Textbook of Psychiatry*, Vol. 2, Williams and Wilkins Company, Baltimore. 1976.

Quick Reference to the Diagnostic Criteria from DSM III. American Psychiatric Association, 1980.

Regensberg, D.J. Objective Social Incontinence, *Nursing R S A*, Vol. 2, No. 1, January 1987.

Cost Effective Quality Services in the Context of the Health Care Crisis: Implications and Opportunities for South African EAPs

Tracy Harper

SUMMARY. South Africa is facing a health care crisis of staggering proportions. The article provides an overview of the South African health care system, an analysis of the current problems and the implications and patented opportunities for EAPs in health care management in South Africa.

INTRODUCTION

It is generally accepted that the EAP cannot remain separate from its economic and socio-political context. Thus, the South African health and mental health care crisis has implications for the workplace and, in turn, for EAPs and EAP practitioners.

EAPs have been established for a variety of reasons, from seeking alternative ways of managing poor performance, with an emphasis on program cost-effectiveness, to giving expression to the concept of "internal" social responsibility. This latter rationale has gained increasing

---

Tracy Harper holds a Bachelor of Social Science Degree in Social Work (1979) and a Bachelor of Arts Honours Degree in Industrial Social Work (1986). She is an executive member of the Institute of Personnel Managements EAP Committee. She is also a consultant in the EAP field and to Riverfield Lodge–a private alcohol and drug clinic.

The author wishes to thank Reg Broekman, General Manager of Lifecare Clinics, Ltd., for his contributions to this article.

attention in the current climate in which business has sought ways to become more socially responsive both towards employees and towards communities in which they operate (du Plessis, 1991).

The focus of intervention may be based on the family, individual, organization or, in some situations, on the community.

Similar to the United States, EAPs are both provider and consumers of service. The majority of the EAPs are dependent on the health and mental health services in the community in order to be effective. The EAP is also in a position to access funds through their host organizations.

Before looking at the implications of the health and mental health care crisis, some introductory comments concerning the former are necessary.

HISTORICAL PERSPECTIVE

South Africa has developed a dual health care delivery system. Those who can afford it (20% of the population) participate in a private health system, while the remainder of the population (80%) are dependent on the State for health care.

South Africa has (historically) a residual welfare system characterized by recognition of differences between races. Those perceived differences were the basis of apartheid (i.e., separateness), the policy of segregation and political and economic discrimination against non-Europeans–principally blacks. The social welfare institutions come into play only when the normal structures of supply, family and market break down. This system is based on the values of economic individualism and free enterprise.

SOUTH AFRICAN HEALTH CARE STRUCTURE

Private health/mental health care is largely funded by employers as part of the package paid to employees. Contributions are made to medical aid societies which distribute the costs of care. Young and healthy employees are subsidizing those who are older or who suffer from chronic or recurrent health problems.

Regulations Governing Providers and Funders

The health industry is one of the most highly regulated industries in the country. Permits have to be obtained to erect a hospital; the number of beds is controlled by the State; detailed building regulations cover every aspect of the hospital building and regulations govern the tariffs which can be charged. It is anything but a free market.

Funding of the private health system is almost totally through the medical aid schemes in respect of private patients. The Workman's Compensation Act and the Motor Vehicles Insurance Act provide funding through insurance for industrial and motor vehicle accidents respectively.

Certain industries, such as the mining industry, provide health and mental health services for their own employees.

Key Actors in Health Care Delivery

The key actors in South Africa's health services are: the State, private hospitals (including the mining industry); private practitioners; medical aids; and insurance companies, who offer hospital top-up schemes.

Relationship Between Actors

The major criticism of the current system of funding in the private health sector is that of "third party payers." In this system, business and employees contribute to a medical aid society which is then legally required to pay the health bills of the employee (and his/her dependents). Neither the doctor nor the patient have any motivation to reduce the costs of care–or even know what the costs are. New legislation on medical schemes will allow medical schemes to differentiate members' contributions based on claims history. This will make those who are elderly or are less healthy bear more of the costs of their care, possibly making health care less affordable and making mental health care less accessible.

SOUTH AFRICAN HEALTH CARE CRISIS

South African health care is currently in a state of deterioration. This has been the combined effect of a global recession and flat or zero economic growth in the economy. Academic hospitals can no longer carry out certain life-saving procedures (e.g., marrow transplants) because of nursing shortages; certain specialists cannot be obtained at current salaries offered by the State–with inevitable consequences for teaching and standards.

The South African government faces overwhelming funding demands for housing, education, job creation, AIDS, etc. There will be no additional funds forthcoming from the state for health services.

Planning of health services has been shockingly fragmented and very poorly done. There has been no defined planning methodology and there is no public reporting.

Attitudes

Various political parties believe a National Health System will solve our health problems. This does not encourage doctors in the private sector to remain in South Africa.

There are serious rifts between the public and private sectors in health services, each side viewing the other as an opponent rather than a resource.

Friction between various professional groups within the medical field prevents the degree of cooperation needed for an efficient system.

The public generally takes medical care for granted and takes no real interest in the costs of the care. There is no incentive for the public to reduce costs within the present system.

Resource Utilization

Generally, there is a lack of health service resources. This is particularly so in mental health services where there is:

- one psychiatrist for every 127,000 of the population;
- one clinical psychologist for every 35,000 of the population;
- one psychiatric nurse per 5,000 population; and
- one social worker per 5,000 population.

The current health services are unequally divided between rural and urban populations, strongly favoring urban populations. For example: "the vast majority of the Johannesburg area's 220 registered clinical psychologists serve the 600,000 white population, resulting in a practitioner ratio of around 1 to 3,000 population (this fits well with the first world ratios). In the homelands, on the other hand, there are just over 20 psychologists registered for a population of around 16 million–a ratio of around one to 800,000 (Freeman, 1991).

Demographics

Health spending in general has been biased towards the white part of the population. In 1987, R600 ($240 U.S.) was spent per capita on (by) whites, while only R150 ($60 U.S.) was spent on (by) blacks. Since blacks represent a large proportion of the population, the difference will be impossible to make up–even over decades.

Besides the deaths caused by the recent violence, the number of injuries has created a tremendous load on the country's health resources. Other epidemics, such as AIDS, will also demand massive funding to control.

Health Care Training

Standards in health care, and particularly in nursing, have declined severely over the last 10 years. Maintenance of standards is going to be one of the greatest challenges to health care in the future South Africa.

The private sector will have to become involved in training health care workers of all descriptions in future. The State will simply not have the necessary financial resources.

Training of health professionals has been mainly directed towards management of first world medical problems. This has been particularly evident in the training of mental health workers who have been trained in treatment modalities which are labor intensive. However, social work training has pioneered the way to a comprehensive practice, better equipped to treat both first and third world problems.

Health Care Alternatives

Models which are presently under consideration are those of HMO and PPO programs. There is also a strong movement towards a national health and welfare system.

At this stage the health care crisis, although entering the business agenda, does not appear to be a priority. However, the union movement is putting more and more pressure on companies to address the health care needs of their employees. The model preferred by the union is the HMO system. However, according to M. Freeman of the Health Care policy unit of the University of the Witwatersrand, the community-union alliance appears to be caught in something of a dilemma. "On the one hand the call has been for business to be more involved in seeing to the needs of employees and providing more and better services for them, but on the other hand, HMOs could be part of a process of further splitting the health services, potentially endangering what the public sector can provide." Mental health care needs are, however, still a low priority on this agenda.

A group personnel administration manager believes employers have a straightforward choice. The "first alternative is to accept a passive role towards health care and health care costs. The implications of this role are rapidly increasing medical aid costs; escalating demands from all strata of employees for additional assistance towards what are perceived as excessive out-of-pocket costs; and continued losses from high sickness rates.

The second alternative is an active role–the employer accepts that health care is an important employee need, perceived to be largely unsatisfied or at least in danger of becoming unsatisfied. He researches and adopts a creative, consultative approach–looking for a range of ways to assist employees to meet their needs'' (Abbott, 1990). It is, however, felt by employers that in adopting an active role they are not assuming full responsibility for the health of the employee. This remains the responsibility of the individual. Employee Assistance Programs are seen as important vehicles through which the active employer can meet a range of employee health and especially mental health needs. Employee Assistance Programs are seen to be a potential growth area.

IMPLICATIONS AND OPPORTUNITIES FOR SOUTH AFRICAN EAPs

If an employer is to address the health and mental health care needs of the organization, a team approach is necessary. Key actors, such as the EAP practitioner, occupational health physician, and nurse, safety, line management, medical aid and insurance must all be involved in addressing policy issues and putting policy into action. Addressing employees' health care costs, the author believes, is going to become increasingly important as employers start feeling the pinch of the rising healthcare costs.

EAPs will have to address their method of service delivery and look at their effectiveness in assisting with the containment of health care costs.

Curative Measures

At a curative level one of the key factors that EAP practitioners are already addressing is the duration and nature of treatment. With limited resources, both financial and human long term treatment is unlikely to be seen as cost-effective (except in the situation of addiction management) and practitioners are moving towards task oriented and results oriented techniques.

As in the U.S., keeping the employees on the job and accessibility of services are becoming increasingly more important issues. Different levels of care for optimum treatment effectiveness will need to be addressed and initial diagnosis and contracting with employee and service provider will be important for quality cost-effective treatment plans. Recently an EAP work group, consisting of EAP practitioners from several large organizations, asked providers of community services to present their services for assessment. Outpatient treatment and on-site services for mental health are likely to be the rule of the game.

The lack of professional resources is likely to result in more group therapy and the development of self-help groups.

EAP practitioners would need to address the effectiveness of their interventions, not only in maintaining productivity levels but also in reducing health care costs. At this stage it would appear that medical aids are skeptical as to the impact EAP treatment systems are having on reducing health care costs. "Before and After" studies, addressing the utilization of sick leave benefits, are likely to be introduced.

The funding of mental health services at present is one of exclusion or setting strict limits by medical aids and insurance. This has resulted from the fear of funders of how to control perceived escalating costs of such illnesses and also an attitude of total self-responsibility towards mental health.

EAPs also have the potential to play a significant role in Managed Health Systems. The HMO and PPO health care models being discussed in South Africa today, appear to be primarily physically based. The author sees no reason why mental health systems cannot become part of these systems.

A family welfare agency and a not-for-profit EAP set up by a mining employee organization already offer in their contracts with companies an HMO-like model of counseling services. A private alcohol and drug clinic (for profit) with its comprehensive fee structure (which does not exist in any other private hospital) and holistic approach to treatment, is looking at adapting various managed care models in its service delivery to EAPs and employers.

The EAP practitioner has the potential to play a vital role in maintaining cost-effective quality services. The adaptation of the U.S. quality cost-effective treatment techniques such as utilization review, case management and claims coordination reviews could prove to be valuable tools. However, training in these techniques would need to be undertaken.

The author feels that strong discount incentives (to make treatment more affordable) should be given to employees who go through EAP systems. The identification of preferred providers and preferred provider agreements could be made with both the public and private sector and could enhance the goal towards cost-effective quality services. In terms of the public service, such agreements would assist in funding of their services in general. Here, the EAP practitioner could assist the employer in negotiating affordable rates, accessibility of services and other services to ensure treatment effectiveness. Through this system a more balanced approach to the funding of mental health services may be achieved.

The continued tendency of medical aids and insurance to ignore alcohol/drug addiction in managed care plans has one commonality "again, the dependent employee remains in turmoil and all partners lose, i.e., the employee, employer, and medical aid/insurer (Schmidt, 1988). Thus, if one is going to manage health benefit costs at a curative level and not shift them the EAP, the employee, the funder of service and the provider of service must interface to bring a balance between funders responsibility, employee responsibility, and providers responsibility."

Resource Limitations

Noting the above, one has to look at it in the light of scarce resources. These resources are not only "scarce," but often inadequately staffed and funded institutions, and historically divided along racial lines. This has implications for quality services for EAPs, since resources to which employees need to be referred may be non-existent, inaccessible or of poor quality. The health care crisis is likely to exacerbate this situation.

With the lack of resources there will be little space for the duplication of resources. Through EAP statistics and feasibility studies, gaps in resources and resources with potential for development need to be identified. EAPs could play a greater role to help guide their organization in the development and implementation of the resources in the communities. This would obviously have benefits for the employer, employees and the community at large.

At a manpower level, EAPs are attempting to identify other persons in the workplace who could assist in providing services and train them sufficiently to be effective in addressing a number of the more primary mental health issues, e.g., linking with resources, financial counseling, communicating company benefits, use of recovering addicts to assist in managing addiction aftercare.

Further, private resources could also be challenged to meet the need more appropriately.

EAP Practitioners Training

With the growth of Employee Assistance Programs, training of EAP practitioners to ensure quality is needed. At present, most practitioners learn on the job. The Executive Committee of Institute of Personnel Management–EAP committee is presently addressing this issue at a national level. It will also create new job opportunities, career paths and manpower.

Prevention/Promotion

With the lack of resources and the expense of curative care, the role of prevention and promotion is growing rapidly. It also forms a common ground between funders of service (e.g., medical aids) and providers of service, with regard to consumers of health/mental health services.

Examples of such services present in South African EAPs include non-smoking groups and campaigns, stress management, substance abuse prevention, retirement planning, managing violence (a presently escalating problem which is impacting on the workplace), weight loss, lifeskills, etc. Medical Aids are sending out educational information on managing one's health more effectively in an attempt to reduce health care costs. One study undertaken by a large organization has shown the cost benefits to the prevention approach.

Organizational and Political Action

At this stage most EAP practitioners are not directly involved in the development of their organization's health and mental health policies. A more active role is likely to occur as employers are faced more and more with health and mental health related issues at the bargaining table.

To date, most EAP practitioners have been passive in their role in identifying and promoting the types of health and mental health services they would envisage for a new South Africa.

It is imperative that representatives of all health professions in South Africa participate in a planning process that will result in a comprehensive, cost-effective and accessible health service. It must not only meet the needs of the population as a whole, but must also be "owned" by the professionals who are part of the delivery system. Without a comprehensive system, the scope and effectiveness of EAPs will be limited.

REFERENCES

Abbot, P. (1990). The role of the employer in healthcare provision, *IPM Journal*, 19-27, October.

Broomberg, J. (1991). Deregulation of medical aid schemes, *IPM Journal*, 11-25, May.

du Plessis, A. (1991). A society in transition: EAPs in South Africa, *EAP Digest*, 35-58, March/April.

Ewing, N.R. (1991). The role of the employer in providing healthcare services. Paper presented at a Conference on Cost Effective Healthcare.

Freeman, M. (1991). How will psychologists fit into the healthcare system in a post-apartheid society? Paper presented at Psychologist Association of South Africa.

Freeman, M. (1991). Providing mental health care. Paper given at IPM Breakfast Seminar on Managed Healthcare.

Schmidt, C.S. (1988). Management by manipulation: The dilemma of managed mental health care, *EAP Digest*, 18-20, July.

Occupational Social Work Education in South Africa

Sello Mkalipe

SUMMARY. This paper describes findings from a survey by the author, of twenty Schools of Social Work in South Africa and the neighboring so-called "Black Homelands." In addition, the study sought to establish the content, scope and objectives of curricula and opportunities for field placement in OSW.

PURPOSE OF STUDY

The study sought to investigate and accumulate information on Occupational Social Work (OSW) training in South Africa with a view to:

- Presenting such data and information to Schools of Social Work in order to motivate them to begin to consider the inclusion of this concentration in their curricula in accordance with the changing nature of the workplace and workforce in South Africa (du Plessis, 1991).
- Presenting this information to community, private and public sectors, including unions, in order for these sectors to realize the significance of this technology of social work and its potential gains for each and all sectors. Convince and encourage employing agents such as universities, the private sector, government, unions and human resources

---

Sello Mkalipe is a doctoral candidate at the Jane Addams College of Social Work, University of Illinois at Chicago. He is formerly a Senior Social Worker in the EAP at the Chamber of Mines of South Africa. His most recent position was Director of an Adult University Education Adjustment program.

He holds an MSW from the University of Denver and an MA from the International College in Los Angeles.

consultants to begin to consider employing occupational social workers.

- Utilize this information for the betterment of the worker, the employer and the workplace.
- Advance the growth of social work in South Africa so that the profession could learn and share uniquely with other countries, in the advancement of this area of social work and the profession in general.

SOCIAL WORK EDUCATION IN SOUTH AFRICA

Social work education and practice in South Africa, in comparison to the USA and Britain, is of relative recent origin and, understandably, still less developed in many areas of training and services delivery. Following the Great Depression during the late twenties and, in response to the findings and recommendations of the First Carnegie Commission on the "Poor Whites Problem" in South Africa, where large numbers of South Africans were devastated by poverty and unemployment, the first program of social work was established to serve the white community at the University of Stellenbosch in 1932.

It is a significant historical footnote that the first head of this program was the late Dr. Hendrick F. Verwoerd, the key architect and arch proponent of the policy of apartheid of forced racial and ethnic separateness in South Africa.

Training for practice in the African community by Africans was established fourteen years later in 1946 at the now-defunct Jan Hoymeyer College of Social Work for Natives, primarily as a result of the philanthropic efforts of the American missionary, Dr. Ray Phillips.

There are presently twenty institutions that are affiliates of the Joint Universities Council on Social Work. These institutions provide training mainly in the generic social work mold throughout the first three years of the BSW with opportunities for specialization in select concentrations at the end of the Bachelor's Degree and at post-Bachelor's levels of study. The most common concentrations are studies in Aging, Disabilities, Child and Family Welfare, Mental Health and School Social Work. Other aspects of the South African way of life that have a bearing on the daily lives of people, e.g., cross-cultural issues, institutional racism, policy and social changes issues, are conspicuously absent in almost all curricula.

In respect of the world of work and, given the need for novel levels and patterns of understanding and tolerance in the workplace, OSW with its attendant techniques for intervention, such as employee assistance programs, has not been significantly considered for inclusion in most social curricula.

TRAINING IN OCCUPATIONAL SOCIAL WORK

Again, by comparative standards, OSW training in South Africa, is a relatively new concept and phenomenon. Almost 70% of respondents conceded unfamiliarity with the concept and, this was notwithstanding the fact that social work training in South Africa has been involved with the preparation of personnel for practice in the workplace since the mid-seventies. As a new addition to the host of concentrations in social work and as a microcosm of a larger body and system of knowledge, OSW training in South Africa can be better examined and understood, against the background of social work in general.

The complexity of the South African society, coupled with the effects of apartheid, have had a skewed and almost inhibiting result on the distribution of training institutions and the growth of the profession in general. Evidence of this may be noted from the geographic and institutional dispersion, characteristics and disparities between these institutions. In South Africa there are certain areas that are generally deemed to be socially and economically backward and non-viable in many respects, and that have been set aside, in terms of the "Homelands Policy," for primary occupation and settlement by the various African ethnic groups. Another outstanding characteristic of these areas is that they are situated far from the hub of mainstream commercial, economic, industrial, and social activities. As a result, social institutions in these areas are generally considered as underdeveloped and wanting in terms of experienced human resources including sufficient financial and social resources (Butler et al., 1977).

As such, reference has been made to "homeland or bush" universities to refer to centers of higher learning that are situated in these areas, as opposed to the term "white universities" that are located in the cities and have been traditionally associated with the white community and prosperity. There are at present six of these "bush universities" and they account for 30% of all Schools of Social Work in South Africa. They accommodate 28% of all social work student registrations. This is in contrast to "white universities" that account for 70% of all schools of social work and account for 72% of all social work student registrations (Table 1).

One revealing aspect from these indices is that the seeming inability of "homeland universities" to attract or accommodate a comparable number of students to "white universities" has compelling implications for both budget and staffing. This is more so in that generally, student populations determine and set limits on areas of study and concentrations, in addition to market demands in communities of interest.

SURVEY METHODOLOGY

Twenty, 7-item questionnaires were mailed to Heads of Schools of Social Work. A reminder was sent seven weeks later to eleven of the schools. Nineteen of the questionnaires were returned for a 95% response rate. Seventy-one percent of the items in the questionnaire served as motivational inquiry for the study and the rest of the items related to whether participating schools would have wished to receive further communication and results from the survey.

TABLE 1

COMPARATIVE DATA ON OVERALL SOCIAL WORK STUDENT REGISTRATIONS IN TRADITIONAL "WHITE" AND TRADITIONAL "BUSH" SCHOOLS OF SOCIAL WORK IN SOUTH AFRICA (1988 SURVEY)

	Traditional White	Traditional Bush
Undergraduate 1 to 4 years of study	2053	1015
Advanced Diploma 1 year of study	40	1
Honors Degree 1 year of study	253	48
Masters Degree Minimum 2 years of study	324	17
Doctoral Degree Minimum 2 years of study	69	5
Totals	2739 (72%)	1096 (28%)

RESULTS

It was learned from the nineteen respondents that students in the OSW concentration throughout the five accredited levels of study, i.e., the four year Bachelor's Degree, the Advanced Diploma in Social Work, the Honours, Masters and Doctoral Degrees, accounted for an average 6% of all registrations in social work (Table 2).

Responses to inquiry into the content and scope of OSW curricula, revealed a lack of understanding by most schools on the essence of OSW as opposed to the traditional industrial work approach. In some instances, the inclination was to equate OSW to industrial social work. Whereas in the field of traditional industrial social work, the focus is on the "employee-as-person" (du Plessis, 1988), with manifest problems such as alcohol and drug abuse (Gustavsson and Balgopal, 1991). OSW takes a more

TABLE 2

COMPARATIVE DATA ON AVERAGE TOTAL STUDENT REGISTRATIONS IN SOCIAL WORK AND OSW STUDENT REGISTRATIONS (1988 SURVEY)

	Total Student Registrations	Total OSW Student Registrations
Undergraduate 1 to 4 years of study	3068 (80%)	178 (5%)
Advanced Diploma 1 year of study	41 (1%)	6 (.15%)
Honors Degree 1 year of study	311 (8%)	9 (.23%)
Masters Degree Minimum 2 years of study	341 (9%)	15 (.39%)
Doctoral Degree Minimum 2 years of study	74 (2%)	6 (.15%)
Totals	3835 (100%)	214 (6%)

expanded approach both in the definition of the area of concern, the workplace, as well as in the content of services delivery (Googins and Godfrey, 1987).

For instance, from a semantic perspective, the term, "occupational," embraces a wider definition of the world of work as opposed to the linear "industrial" term. In addition, OSW perceives the employee, management, the workplace, the family, unions (in the case where they apply), and the community as a total holistic system of units that share a symbiotic relationship and have the potential to sustain each other.

This approach to OSW seemed to elude most respondents and, among those schools that were considering the inclusion of OSW in their curricula, a need was expressed, to consult experts who would assist them in OSW planning, designing, teaching and on-going evaluation.

Responses to inquiry into course contents and the scope of curricula in OSW revealed a host of issues that were offered by schools. These have been categorized into following major areas: the Field and Context for Industrial Social Work Practice, Unemployment and Benefits, Pre-Retirement and Retirement Issues, Personnel Work, Problem-Solving Approaches in Social Work, Trade and Labor Issues, Social Responsibility and Social Development Programs, the Workmen's Compensation Act and Benefits, Vocational Guidance and Counseling, Sociology of the Workplace, and Research Methods. These areas of study are offered mainly at the fourth year of the Bachelor's Degree and the Advanced Diploma level including the Honors Degree level, as prescribed course content. Students are expected to submit as well a mini-thesis of lesser content and scope for the Master's and Doctoral Degree expectations on any one of the above issues in fulfillment of the requirements for the award of the Degree.

Requirements for the Master's and Doctoral Degrees are confined to the selection of an approved topic, a minimum of two years preoccupation with research and the final submission and defense of the thesis. This preference in postgraduate standards would seem to be the norm throughout all South African universities and as approved by South African Post Secondary Education (SAPSE) standards. This is in contrast to procedure in most countries, notably the USA, where postgraduate programs warrant pursuit of prescribed course work jointly with the submission and defense of a thesis at the Doctoral level.

A possible explanation for this dissimilarity in standards would be, that while the U.S. master's and doctoral programs are relatively liberal in terms of their entrance qualifications, where entering students for postgraduate studies may possess a Bachelor's or Master's Degree as the case may be, and that may not have any relevance to social work; institutions in South Africa insist that entering Master's and Doctoral candidates should possess undergraduate or Honors training and certification in their intended fields of study. The study revealed as well that most course contents that are commonly found in OSW curricula in U.S. institutions were not readily found in OSW curricula in South Africa.

To name but a few, these course units would include conceptual frameworks for organizational theory in OSW, essential elements for designing OSW and EAPs, employee and family outreach efforts, training skills for managers and supervisors in the early identification and referral of troubled employees, the role of the social worker and counselor in OSW and EAPs, the role of unions in OSW and EAPs, studies in alcohol and drug abuse including policy issues and research.

Inquiries into field placements, frequency and durations of such placements, revealed that though scarce, internship opportunities were available in the fourth year of the Bachelor's Degree, Advanced Diploma, and the Honors level. In all instances, field placements were coordinated with the student's elected field of study, coursework and the mini-research.

Students are generally placed for an average and random three days per week or in block placements of between three to five days per week for between three to six months. This is usually between March and late October and represents the span between a month after entry into the program and usually, a month before the final examinations. In all instances, the field practice course, while closely related to coursework, is an independent course with its own credit load and grade. From a related survey into private and public sector involvement in OSW internships (Mkalipe, 1988), it was established that in most instances, placements were confined to clinical interventions with troubled employees and alcohol and drug abuse problems.

Data on estimates of students who were exclusive to the OSW concentration throughout all levels of study, revealed a concentration of 83% in the undergraduate program notably at the fourth year level, 3% in the Advanced Diploma, 4% at the Honors level and 7% and 3% respectively at the Master's and Doctoral levels. This would imply that a great proportion of OSW students are absorbed by employment after the Bachelor's Degree and in relation to the "white/homelands" universities continuum, the situation is pronouncedly skewed. Ninety-seven percent of students in "homeland universities" are either absorbed by the workplace or simply do not bother to take up postgraduate studies in these institutions or prefer to pursue their studies in other universities (Table 3).

Since the overall objective of most schools is to prepare students for work in clinical intervention, great emphasis is laid on problem-solving skills and counseling services. As part of their objectives, most schools indicated that their students are also expected to possess insights into the workplace and ethics of work. To this end, emphasis was placed as well on field placement and the vital function of supervised practica.

CONCLUSION

The history of social work and its relationship to industry and business in South Africa has been increasing steadily since the Sixties. It was recorded that by the close of 1987, almost 200 practitioners would have been identified in the field of industrial social work and welfare work nationwide (du Plessis, 1988). Core areas of service have centered around welfare services for employees and their families, counseling for troubled workers usually with alcohol and drug abuse problems and service retirement and unemployment benefit schemes.

What is generally considered to be the ecological perspective in OSW (Gustavsson and Balgopal, 1991) and that transcends the linear "employee service model" (Shank, 1985) has been omitted by most schools in their approach to training social work for workplace practice.

In the ecological mold, students are expected to intervene at all levels of the organization and assume a variety of roles. These may include the roles of advocate, trainer, broker, consultant, community planner, administrator, mobilizer and other roles, depending on the nature of the work as presented (Shank, 1985).

Essentially, curricula are generally considered as social, political and cultural statements. To this end therefore, curricula do not only deal with the structure of that which has to be taught and learned (Guzzetta, 1984), rather, curricula should be seen to represent the tide of life in any society. In this regard, social work curricula in South Africa ought to begin to appreciate the need to keep abreast with social, political, and cultural developments in that country.

One of the arenas in which these developments have been taking place, is in the workplace. Recent reforms in that country have resulted in the abolition of discriminatory legislation such as the Job Reservation Act, whereby certain sectors of the population were precluded from taking up

TABLE 3

COMPARATIVE DATA ON OVERALL OSW STUDENT REGISTRATIONS, IN TRADITIONAL "WHITE" AND TRADITIONAL "HOMELANDS" UNIVERSITIES

	Traditional White	Traditional Homelands
Undergraduate*		
1 to 4 years of study	109	69
Advanced Diploma		
Minimum 1 year of study	6	-
Honors Degree		
Minimum 1 year of study	7	2
Masters Degree		
Minimum 2 years of study	15	-
Doctoral Degree		
Minimum 2 years of study	6	-
Totals	143 (67%)	71 (33%)

*While specializations are generally confined to the post-graduate levels of study, some institutions prefer to streamline students into areas of specialization at the undergraduate level but preferably at the fourth year of study.

jobs that were reserved for other population groups. As a result, relaxation in legislation has resulted in novel challenges and demands for previously excluded groups. In the process, a host of adjustment and performance problems may be experienced by most people. In turn, this has had an impact on their productivity and job performance.

For instance in a document released by the Human Science Research Council on behalf of the mining industry in South Africa, it was revealed that more than 25% of mine workers suffer from personal and interpersonal problems, with 20% of them experiencing what may be considered as serious problems (Chamber of Mines, 1988). The mining industry is but one of the instances where dramatic changes have been experienced by most workers. For instance African mineworkers can now qualify and be licensed as Blasters (setting and exploding dynamite) and work side-by-side with their colleagues from other racial groups. This is in contrast to the days when the holding of blast certificates and the prerogative for this trade was reserved for racial groups other than Africans.

The nature of social work in a changing and developing society such as South Africa, demands of the field of social work to be representative of a much wider variety of skills and training areas as opposed to when the society was restrictive and highly regulated. To this end, students need to be exposed to novel and varied issues relating to the overall well-being of individuals and their families, including the society and its subsystems in general.

Occupational Social Work is one of those training areas that has to be considered by academia in South Africa if the quality of life of business, commerce, industry, labor, the individual and the community is to be improved.

REFERENCES

Butler, J., Rotberg, R.I., & Adams, J. (1977). *The black homelands in South Africa.* University of California Press.

Chamber of Mines of South Africa. (1988). *Gold and human beings.* Human Resources Development.

du Plessis, A. (1988). Industrial social work practice: Course Outline. (Unpublished). University of the Witwatersrand, School of Social Work.

du Plessis, A. (1991). A society in transition: EAP's in South Africa. *EAP Digest.* March/April.

Googins, B., & Godfrey, J. (1987). *Occupational social work.* Englewood Cliffs, N.J.: Prentice-Hall, Inc.

Gustavsson, N.S., & Balgopal, P.R. (1991). Training of social workers in work settings: Response of the academia. *Employee Assistance Quarterly* 6(4), 79-89.

Guzetta, C.J. (1984). Model for analysis of program curricula in social work education. Paper presented at the IASSW Congress, Montreal (Unpublished).

Maiden, R.P., & Hardcastle, D. (1986). Social work education: Professionalizing EAP's. *EAP Digest.* November/December, 63-66.

Maiden, R.P. (1991). Course outline: Principles and practices in employee assistance/managed care programs. University of Illinois at Chicago, Jane Addams College of Social Work. (Unpublished).

Mkalipe, S.J. (1988). Survey among a random sample of 100 companies in the PWV area, on the use of occupational social workers and the placement of students in OSW. (Unpublished).

Mkalipe, S.J. (1988). Questionnaire to determine the extent to which occupational social work (OSW) is part of social work programs and content in South African universities and the neighboring states. (Unpublished).

Shank, B. (1985). Considering a career in occupational social work? *EAP Digest.* July/August, 55-61.